LIFE & WORK

A MANAGER'S SEARCH FOR MEANING

Other Avon Books by
James A. Autry

LOVE AND PROFIT

LIFE & WORK

A MANAGER'S SEARCH FOR MEANING

JAMES A. AUTRY

AVON BOOKS ◆ NEW YORK

The poems "Things Done Right" and "Death in the Family" first appeared in *Nights Under a Tin Roof.*

AVON BOOKS
A division of
The Hearst Corporation
1350 Avenue of the Americas
New York, New York 10019

The William Morrow edition contains the following Library of Congress Cataloging in Publication Data:
Autry, James A.
  Life and work: a manager's search for meaning / James A. Autry.
    p.   cm.
  1. Management—Philosophy.   2. Management—Poetry.
  3. Management—Anecdotes.   I. Title.
HD38.A838   1994   93-36186
658—dc20   CIP

First Avon Books Trade Printing: May 1995

AVON TRADEMARK REG. U.S. PAT. OFF. AND IN OTHER COUNTRIES, MARCA REGISTRADA, HECHO EN U.S.A.

Printed in the U.S.A.

OPM 10 9 8 7 6 5 4 3 2 1

*For my loved ones—
colleagues, friends, family—
and most especially, Sally*

Acknowledgments

Writing this book has been more difficult than I thought it would be.

When Adrian Zackheim, the editor at William Morrow who guided me through the publication of *Love and Profit*, said he'd like me to try a book of "letters" and, though they should be focused through the viewpoint of a businessman, they could be on any subject, I thought, *Wow! What a great assignment.*

But then the questions began. What subjects? How personal should they be? How long should the letters be? Should they be to real people or fictional people? If to real people, how do I avoid invading their privacy, or how do I respect their sensibilities on these subjects?

And as I plunged further and further into the book, I faced the great overriding question every author faces: Who gives a damn about what I have to say anyway? Also, doesn't this format become a bit tedious?

Finally, after reading my completed book of "letters," Adrian came forth with a less structured, more flexible format, as well as a new title. For that I am grateful.

Through it all, Rafe Sagalyn, my agent, was encouraging.

And as always, my friends—particularly my writer friends—kept me plugging away. Thanks first to Mel Wilk. Then a special thanks to Betty Sue Flowers, who touched the manuscript here and there with her magic pencil. And to Michelle Urry, whose ear is ever sharp and clear.

I also can't overlook the font of remembrance and information shared in many ways by David Jordan.

During the past year, I have spent many inspiring and informative hours working with senior executives and the employees of their companies. Some of these experiences are reflected in several letters throughout the book.

Four of those executives have been especially important to my own learning and growth: Tom Gould of Younkers, Inc.; Doug Greene and Cinda Johnson of New Hope Communications; and Matt Handbury of Murdoch Magazines, Sydney, Australia. Thank you all.

I would be remiss in not acknowledging the thousands of people who bought and read *Love and Profit* and the letters they wrote in support of it and, by extension, in support of this book.

Let me not fail to recognize also my associate Debbie McCarroll, without whose dedication and competence I could never have found the time to write a single word.

I thank my sons: Jim, who in his struggles and experiments with the management of a rock band, *Made Ya Look,* helped me frame some thoughts about the difficulties of "communal management"; Rick, attorney and computer whiz, mathematician and philosopher, who contributed directly with ideas of his own; and Ronald, third-grader (by the time this is published), and a frequent character in these letters.

By this time, the reader realizes that I was only the writing instrument of this book; the inspiration and material came from many sources. If, as in *Love and Profit,* the byline was to be shared, however, it should be shared with my wife, Sally. She has read, commented, critiqued, and offered alternative ideas throughout the writing and editing of the manuscript. Though I have not always received those comments with equanimity, I have always accepted them with gratitude and love.

Contents

Introduction

The question I struggled with for many years goes something like this: How can I keep my life and my work properly separated?

It was the wrong question.

The right question, which I did not begin to ask until about 1980, is How can I keep my life and my work properly integrated? Because I was a senior corporate manager by the time I engaged the right question, I naturally had to include the question of properly integrating into both my life and work my employees, the people who were put in my care day to day.

The philosophies and theories and techniques for achieving this integration of work and life, of employees and family, led to my book *Love and Profit: The Art of Caring Leadership* (William Morrow, 1991). Publication of the book put me on yet another path of discovery, traveling and speaking and consulting for companies and groups in this country and abroad.

What has astonished me is the widespread recognition by businesspeople of the need to accept and respond to constant change. This in itself has led to a wave of change sweeping business, with company executives finding, more and more, that regardless of organizational structure, of special programs or processes, the only thing that really works in bringing about significant, long-lasting, positive change is a working environment in which people can integrate their work and their lives in ways that provide meaning and fulfillment and dignity and worth. Without such an environment, the rest of it is doomed; within such an environment, a company can achieve the "impossible."

The environment, of course, is the primary responsibility of management, most especially senior management.

Because creating this environment was the subject of *Love and Profit,* I speak about these things to managers around the country. I am asked a lot of questions, some of them skeptical if not cynical, but most of them truly in quest of answers about the everyday stuff of managing.

Many of these questions have led me to write the material in this book. Other questions, about both work and life, have come from my friends and family. Those too have I addressed here. Then there are letters and essays and poems I simply felt impelled to write as a result of my own internal questions.

The result is a collection of writings on a wide array of subjects, but all generally addressing the larger issues of finding meaning in life and work, of properly integrating the two, of achieving that exquisite balance within the professional and the personal while honoring their intense and inseparable emotional interrelationship. It is because of this interrelationship, with each area of life constantly informing the other, that I insist we must find the balance "in" and not "between."

Regarding the letters, I have chosen, for reasons of convenience, to address most of them to two "conglomerate" characters: a fictitious son named Art, who is still in his first job, and a fictitious daughter named Clare, who has been at it a while and is now in middle management. A third fictitious character, a niece named Sue, receives a letter from time to time. Sue is younger, just graduating from high school, and has a lot of doubt and criticism about business.

A few of the letters, for obvious reasons, are addressed to my real sons, Jim, Rick, and Ronald.

Because of my background as a corporate executive and my present work on boards of directors and as a consultant for companies, I have tried throughout this book to focus my viewpoint through the prism of a businessperson, always keeping in mind the impact that business has on these subjects, and vice versa. But I confess that some of these words are purely and simply those of a father to his children.

I had some difficulty dividing this book into logical and separate sections. You, the reader, surely will find things in one section that could as easily fit into another. In a way, that's just fine, and I hope you'll let those observations serve as a metaphor about the difficulty of making separations between life and work.

—J.A.A.
Des Moines, Iowa

In dwelling, live close to the ground.
In thinking, keep to the simple.
In conflict, be fair and generous.
In governing, don't try to control.
In work, do what you enjoy.
In family life, be completely present.
—LAOTZU, *Tao-te Ching*
A new English version
by Stephen Mitchell, copyright 1988

Without work all life goes rotten. But when work is soulless
life stifles and dies.
—ALBERT CAMUS

Part One

Working, Managing, and Leading

Success and the Fear of Being Found Out

Dear Art:

Perish the thought that people of accomplishment and success never feel insecure. To the contrary, it is often those feelings of insecurity, those wounds, that push people to strive so hard for success and, many times, to achieve so much.

I had lunch a couple of years ago with a friend who is a senior vice president of media relations and advertising for one of the largest companies in this country. We have become close over the years, and have learned to break the old seller/client barriers and talk about real life.

At this lunch, he stopped eating abruptly, put down his knife and fork and asked, "Do you ever get the feeling that one day they are going to come into your office and say, 'Okay, Autry, we found out about you'?"

"Yes, yes," I said, almost shouting, "I frequently get that feeling. You, too?"

He nodded, and we both began to laugh.

"It's as if we're still the little boys playing with the big boys," he said. "We don't really belong here, do we?"

"Of course not. In the big office with the big salary and the big title and the perks? Of course not. That's for the big boys."

"You know what this tells us?" he continued.

I knew, but I could not find the exact words. He did it for me:

"There are no big boys, only us little boys."

Then we talked about the insecurities that made both of us feel that somehow we were out of our depth, that we did not really belong in this big-time business world. We told stories of our childhoods and our disappointments, of our parents and their disappointments with us, of school days and striving to be part of the group.

Neither of us had played football, which was a big thing where we each grew up. We hadn't been popular with other kids, especially girls. We hadn't had cars. The real wounds, of course, had much deeper causes than those surface reasons, still those things had brought their own disappointments, which somehow we knew we still carried.

Well, I do not want to fall into psychobabble and a confessional about my fears and insecurities. Suffice it to say that none of us should assume that those whom we admire, who are successful, who it seems to us live to a standard of accomplishment we can never attain are as happy, as secure, as self-assured, or as fulfilled as they seem.

Also—and I am guilty of this one—we should not imbue them with superhuman powers which, stated another way, is our *expectation* of their superhuman powers. And we should not confuse our ideals with those who simply try to live and express those ideals. It is not fair to them, nor is it fair to ourselves.

So don't think that success is out of your reach because you perceive that you don't have the "stuff" of successful people. And don't let those people, who often are driven as my friend and I were to overcome the wounds of their childhood by "proving" their worth according to the world's definitions of success, define success for you.

Define it by your own standards, by what it seems important inside yourself to accomplish. Then go to it, realizing that if you can achieve satisfaction and fulfillment in the very effort of trying, rather than in the accomplishment of *everything* you set out to do, you will have achieved 99 percent of the value of what success really means.

With love,
Dad

Listen for the Stories

Dear Clare:

It sounds as if you learned a lot in the workshop on "active listening," and I can't think of a skill in need of more development among managers.

The next issue, of course, is when you're listening, what are you listening for? What are you hoping to hear?

The answers can range all over the place, and most of them would be correct: ideas for product improvement or process improvement; criticism and ideas about working conditions or compensation or benefits; comments about management style and how it helps or inhibits the work; and so on.

But there's something perhaps more important than all this, something less about the process of work and more about the community of work: A manager should be listening for the *stories*.

Just as our stories bond us in family or in friendship, it is our stories that bond us in the community of work. And it is stories which create the bonding mythology of any organization, including a corporation. Several authors have written on this in the past year or so, and there are scholars now studying and cataloging the stories of various companies.

The most eloquent person I know on this subject is Warren Neel, dean of the College of Business Administration at the University of Tennessee. Dean Neel has spent quite some time at the Saturn Corporation, and it is probably no coincidence that Saturn's very successful advertising campaign features "stories" of satisfied customers.

I believe the manager has to listen for and learn the stories, and I believe the manager then has to pass them along, adding her own along the way. In effect, the manager becomes also a *custodian of the stories,* which I hold to be as important as any other management responsibility.

And you have to pay attention, or you may not even recognize them as stories. It would be easy if the stories were all about momentous, earth-shaking events, but they won't be. To the contrary, most of the stories that bind us together, that make our work real every day, are the "little" stories, the personal stories about incidents or episodes, about humorous escapades, about goof-ups as well as triumphs. They will be about the time a small group went against the system and accomplished something great; or about the time management pushed something down their throats and it didn't work ("We could have told them, but they didn't want to listen"); or about a bang-up party; or about winning the softball tournament against the real macho team from production.

No matter how insignificant they may seem, always remember that these stories, woven together, are a powerful part of that fabric we call the culture of a company or, put another way, the community in which the company's work is done.

You know I can't end this letter without some stories of my own, and because I'm writing this just before Christmas, I am remembering those days when the company I worked for always gave its five-year service watches during the holiday season.

This ceremony took place in individual departments as a contingent of senior corporate management harrumphed its way from place to place, calling the names, presenting the watches, and receiving the appropriate expressions of gratitude according to the "way things are done."

But I was part of the creative group at the time, and we were not much taken with the "way things are done." Our leader was the editor of one of our magazines and, as department head, always had a role in the presentations.

I remember one Christmas when he was to present a five-year watch to our senior garden editor. As the corporate officers looked on, the editor said to the garden editor, "Tony, it took you twenty years to develop a green thumb, but after only three weeks with this cheap watch, you'll have a green wrist."

The place flew apart in laughter. I don't know the true reaction of those senior VPs, but to their credit, they laughed as hard as everyone else. And that story went into the oral history of our department.

This bit of irreverence led to a new tradition: From that time on, the creative group's watch recipients were to prepare some kind of skit which they were to present "in appreciation" of their new watches. During the year I was to receive my watch, there was a reorganization at the top of the company, a result of which was to add several new vice presidents to the list.

At the same time, one of the ongoing sources of discontent was the lack of air conditioning in our building. So I sang a carol to the tune of "The Twelve Days of Christmas," with the closing line, "Give us fewer vice presidents and more air conditioning."

Another company tradition was to give everyone a canned ham and a basket of fruit and nuts. In fact, most of us thought it a generous act by the company, but everyone jokingly referred to the ham as our Christmas bonus. Naturally, during one watch ceremony, one of the recipients sang a carol to the tune of "Deck the Halls with Boughs of Holly." It began, "Can the ham, we'll take the cash, tra la la la la, la la la la."

Some of the stories seem almost silly, like fraternity or sorority stuff, so why do I remember them, and what makes them important? Only this: To all who remember them and all who hear them, they convey a sense of how we were together, how open the company was, and how intact its sense of humor was. They tell us something about what it was like to work there at that time, and they provide what I think of as a "thread of foolishness" connecting the young employees of those days with the young employees of these days. It's another way of saying, perhaps proving: "You see, we older manager types weren't always so stuffy."

But not all the stories were irreverent, nor were they all humorous. Sometimes, they were touching.

There was the time our CEO was giving us a year-end report. He was so proud of what we had accomplished, he broke down.

Once during a problem at the printing plant, a group of us went there to help out, even though we were not qualified to do anything very important.

There was the sales conference with a real "Come to Jesus" revival-meeting kind of finale, tapping into our almost religious feelings about our work and inspiring us to go forth and do even better.

I remember a food photograph that we propped and set up in the trunk of a rental car. It ended up on the cover of the magazine and became a best-seller.

There was the older, very hard-working staffer who at the end of a tough day would always cheer us up by saying, "I'm ready to lay aside the cares of the day and let mirth reign unrestrained."

And the art director who kept his office filled with his whimsical junk sculpture, almost like our own gallery.

There were the slide-show glitches during the big sales presentations; the hot summer afternoon "staff meetings" at a little beer-and-sandwich place, where we probably accomplished more than if we'd met in the un-air-conditioned conference room; and always, the times we beat the deadline or made the sale or cut the costs beyond anyone's—even our own—expectations.

So listen to the stories, Clare, and create your own, for they become the history of what you and your coworkers choose to do together.

And another thing: Always try to let mirth reign un-restrained.

With love,
Dad

SEASONS

Did the year begin with the budget
or with the first forecast of the fiscal?
I don't know, it was such a blur
of meetings and computer runs,
but it was a time of excitement and expectation,
as all new years should be,
when we realized that the old was behind us,
for better or worse,
for increased earnings or declines,
and we would take our bonuses or our lumps
and move on to the next year,
another choice, a new beginning,
a chance to improve, to grow,
and with just one breakthrough
and some help from the economy,
even to be great.

Then it was late summer,
the calm before the storm,
when meetings were harder to schedule,
softball and volleyball leagues in full swing,
putting managers and employees on the company's
only truly level playing field,
the popcorn and beer celebrations of winners and losers,
when hierarchy and status seemed to fade away.
It was not the weather but the meetings
that signaled the coming of fall,
with every conference and trade show and sales meeting

squeezed between the start of school and Thanksgiving
and in the middle of all that
the end of the first quarter
with the earnings report that told us
whether we could breathe easy and keep pushing
or cut costs and keep pushing.

The holidays, beginning as always
with homemade cookies and candy
and gatherings at the coffeepot,
gave us reason to be a community again.
There were celebrations that melted the barriers,
often with the help of cognac in the coffee
or vodka in the punch,
and on that last day before Christmas,
parties traveled from office to office
where earnest young up-and-comers told the boss
how to run the company
while those who understood
how far barriers really drop
turned their attention to caroling.

We lived the belief that it was impossible
to start anything during the holidays,
so in January we discovered our desks
covered with call slips,
invoices for all those promises we made
to get to whatever it was
"after the first of the year."
And we found ourselves snowed into airports
and cities where we did not want to be,

always on a Friday night,
standing in line to use the phone
to say we would not be home again.

By this time
we knew how the year was going
and if things were good,
an energy filled the place,
a spirit that we could do even better,
could beat our budget.
If things were bad,
we would tell ourselves it was not too late,
that we could still pull it out.

February and March brought budgeting and planning,
the season of mixed messages,
of endless revisions and complaints,
"We don't even know how this year will turn out,
much less three years from now for Godsake."
But somehow it gave form
to our best expectations of ourselves
and when the numbers were in and the plan ready,
we waited our turn in the barrel,
our presentation to the CEO
and his management group who,
like the men on the Dutch Masters cigar box,
seemed always sitting in doubt and judgment
of our best work, yet at the same time
giving us a common adversary.
Like the orals in college,
the promotion review board in the military,

it was more than anything their chance
to show they were still in touch
with things they left behind years ago.
The new among us tried to be perfect
while the rest of us
always left a few things
for the Dutch Masters men to find and change
else they find and change
something important
which, when it happened,
would send us scrambling for other numbers
and new rationales,
throwing us off rhythm and out of balance
for another month.

With the budget done and the plan set,
we raced toward the end of the year,
the closing, the shifting of costs and revenues
from one fiscal to another,
depending on where we needed the earnings
and, of course, on what the auditors would allow.

Then we closed the circle,
celebrating good years and bad,
picnicking and partying,
sneaking away early on beautiful days,
vacationing with our families,
and plunging into the summer games
as if there were no tomorrow.

Just What Is the Right Thing?

Managers frequently ask me about their moral dilemmas at work. They want to do the right thing, but the answers don't come easily. In fact, sometimes even the definitions of "right thing" don't come as easily as critics outside business insist they should.

We rarely get the easy choices—wrong versus right, good versus evil—that seem so apparent to those who are not engaged in management every day. Too often the choices are between the better of two "rights" or the lesser of two "wrongs." This is true whether the choice involves the rights and needs of one member of the group versus the rights and needs of the group as a whole, or the "right price" to a customer versus the "right return" on the owner's investment. This is to say nothing of the increasing pressures of environmental concerns, safety concerns, hiring practices, advertising claims, and on and on.

Sooner or later, the question we all have to face in life as well as work, is, What will I not do *ever*? or Where do I draw the line beyond which I absolutely will not go?

Some answers are easy. Murder, for instance. Of course. What about theft? Embezzlement? Those are still easy *no's* for most of us. But few of us can say we won't break the law; we do it every time we speed, which for most drivers I know is frequently.

Then we come to things like lying, and here the waters of moral behavior get murkier.

In my consulting work with companies, I try to begin

with what I call "values workshops." The format is simple, but the process can be excruciating because it requires that executives, middle managers, and employees confront together the gaps between the values that they say should exist in the company and the values that actually do exist.

We examine institutional values and personal values, both in the context of the workplace. We begin with values as we would like them to be. For institutional values, I ask participants to complete this statement: "I want to work for a company that values X." For personal values, it's "I want to work with people who value X."

That's always the easy part. Then comes an examination of values as they are. The first statement is, "*This* company values X," and the second statement is, "*These* people value X."

The contrast between the two is where, as they say, the rubber meets the road. And the examination can be a very difficult reality adjustment for the participants, especially the senior management people.

But they ain't seen nothin' yet, because just as soon as this list gets established—which may take days—we begin to look at how even our seemingly most cherished values begin to distort when pushed too far.

Everyone agrees, for instance, that honesty is a desired value. It is often expressed as "honesty and truth-telling."

Another value inevitably will be "mutual respect." It may be stated as "treating people with integrity," which can encompass honesty and respect. "Sensitivity" appears frequently on the list.

But what about the person who is so honest that he or

she is simply tactless, the person who is blunt to the point of insult?

Usually, everyone in my workshops has worked with someone who has this trait, someone who when critiqued about it will always say, "I'm just being honest." Is that honesty or is that using the guise of honesty to bludgeon another person with our most effective everyday weapon, words?

At this point, you might agree with my workshop participants that the values of sensitivity or respect for others should on occasion mitigate "honesty."

At another phase of my work, the group examines how the company may say it values something then will give incentives, through direction or through financial reward, to its people to do something apparently in violation of that expressed value.

In working with senior management people, I find many who will commit a multitude of "small sins" for the sake of business advantage, both institutionally and personally. Airlines offend me particularly because they are the only business I know that has institutionalized lying to its customers as a normal way of doing business. For instance, they purposely will lie about the status of a delayed flight until it's too late to change to a competing airline.

What this says is that the perceived need for business success justifies dishonesty, or mitigates the value of honesty. The irony is that not one top leader in these companies would consider himself or herself a "dishonest person."

My role is not to rub people's noses in their foibles.

And my intent here is not to complain about the short-comings I see in business, because I see so many offsetting good examples: companies that make fine products, advertise them honestly, and stand behind them. These companies usually are the ones that provide good results for all their "stakeholders"—owners, employees, customers, vendors, and the community at large. And I see companies that define their business mission to include support of social causes, of the arts, of special community projects. I also see business leaders doing the same thing.

No, my purpose is to suggest that we all must constantly be aware of the pressures pushing us toward those things we say we will not do, and we all must understand that the things we say we hold true—our values—can and do frequently counterbalance one another in ways that may seem at times in conflict.

The problem is that we businesspeople are very good at kidding ourselves, at rationalizing our way into the best "business decision." This means, of course, that the first challenge is, as always, being honest with ourselves.

Which then leads to the only choice I believe we have: to *behave with integrity,* by which I mean, always examine and search for the path, the action, the deeds that most align with our beliefs, with what we determine within ourselves we will and will not do *ever.*

Everybody's Talkin'
About Leadership

Dear Art:

You are right in saying that the country seems to fall for the politician who has a clear understanding of only the first step in a ten-step problem. But it's true not only of some politicians, but of some business "leaders," as well.

In business, we seem to fall for the "leader" who has the short-term answer, who wants to take all those "decisive" actions to "turn this company around and get it moving again." (Sounds a lot like a politician, doesn't it?) This usually means improving the short-term earnings.

While often falling for the short-term thinkers, we in business still devote a lot of words, written and spoken, to the subject of leadership: how to train leaders and how to become leaders.

You see, Art, leadership has become all the rage these days. It has taken the place of "intrepreneuring," excellence, superior customer service, lean and mean organizations, and total quality management as the business topic of the moment.

Those who scan history in search of lessons for today have discovered that everyone from Socrates to Attila the Hun to Lao-tzu to Jesus seems to have written or spoken at least a few wisdoms about leadership.

Even I've done it.

Yet, when I was running a large operating group for a Fortune 500 company, I used to say that while everyone is talking about leaders, I will settle for some highly competent managers. To my mind, management is a noble calling as well as a sacred trust in which the well-being of employees is put in the manager's care during most of their waking hours.

But I have become persuaded that we in business do need to recognize the difference between the technocratic manager whose focus is systems and organization and control, and the humanistic manager whose focus is people and their support and care and well-being. Perhaps the best way to start distinguishing that difference is, indeed, in the use of the words *leader* and *leadership,* instead of *manager* and *management.*

There's a great deal more to the change than a simple change of vocabulary, however. It's not as if a manager wakes up in the morning and says, "Well, I've got to go be a leader today; I've got to enunciate a vision, walk around a bit, assure alignment, empower people, and so on."

Nonsense.

I know nothing about political leadership, but most of the real work of being a leader in business is in the sum of a hundred little interactions every day.

I've known managers who became irritated that people—their employees—kept interrupting them, kept bringing up all that trivia when they, the managers, needed to get back to managing (whatever that was).

As a senior manager, I have had to refocus those managers by saying, in effect, "Just a minute. All those daily exchanges add up to what you are supposed to be doing most of the time. The biggest challenge of the leader is, without checking on people or making their decisions for them, *in paying attention* to everything, being consistent and focused in every situation, listening to everyone's concerns—yes, including their 'trivia.'"

We know that the techniques of management can be taught, but can leadership be taught? That's the question everyone struggles with.

My answer starts at the other end of the interaction, because this I know: *Leadership can be learned.*

I also know this: The learning of leadership begins as an interior process, the first step of which is self-awareness. The second step is accepting that control is only an illusion.

In my observations of many top business executives, I find much nostalgia for the old command-and-control model of running a business. I know one CEO who was interested in my becoming a consultant for his company, but it was abundantly clear that he wanted me to "fix" his company's culture, then he'd take it from there. I'm afraid his concept of leadership is not unusual. It says, "I can be a good leader if only someone will train the employees on how to follow."

That's the old technocratic "management" maybe, but it's not leadership. The leader has to be among the people, present through every endeavor; accessible, a resource; and, as others before me have said, a "servant."

I recall a quote from an interview with a high-ranking military officer who was decrying the emergence of "management" as the Pentagon hot topic back in the seventies. "Hell," the officer said, "you can't *manage* a bunch of soldiers into risking their lives for their friends and country. You've got to *lead* them."

Of course, in business, the risks are not of violent death; still, there are great risks in business, and the nature of management as it has been practiced for far too many years in America has been to manage the risk-takers right out of our companies.

I need not belabor those same old issues about "empowering people," "praising risk-takers," and "rewarding failure." It has been said too much already.

What has not been said is that, while those currently hip phrases roll off the tongues of thousands of managers throughout America, like a new liturgy, it is very rare to find a company in which these things are actually happening.

But they do exist. I've seen them for myself, and I have this observation: When you find a company in which people feel empowered, in which employees at the lowest levels are making decisions for themselves, in which people are taking risks without fear, innovating, improvising, yet still attuned to how their work fits with everyone else's, do two things:

1. Look around carefully. You'll find a leader there somewhere.

2. Apply for a job, because there's a good chance you can be a leader there, too.

Love,
Dad

A Visual Aid
for Caring Leadership

Shortly before *Love and Profit* was published, I wrote an article for a Meredith Corporation internal publication entitled *The Manager*. In it, I summarized the general thesis of the forthcoming book.

Soon after, I received through interoffice mail a note and the diagram on page 42 from a man whom I considered to be a leading-edge thinker in the human resources department. He is Ken Mishoe, director of personnel at Meredith.

Ken criticized me for not going far enough in the article: "If we are indeed at a turning point (and we are) we must move from anticipation to preparation. . . . I can't resist attaching my own quick, two-dimensional visualization."

It strikes me as brilliant, and I hope managers everywhere slip it into the top drawers of their desks and study it from time to time. In fact, this should be posted on the bulletin boards of every human resources department in the country.

It requires no special insight to see where the true leaders fit on this chart: squarely in Sector I. The person who sees himself or herself as a resource both for others and for the organization will be perceived as a leader *even if that person does not now hold a management title.*

The leader's opposite resides in Sector III, caring mostly for self and very little for organization or others. Some of these people naturally choose this position, I'm

MANAGERS AND RELATIONSHIPS

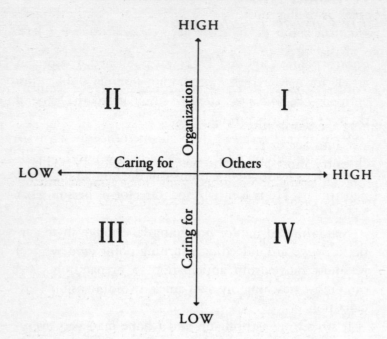

KEY:

Sector I: Managers who are "called"; Lovers; Ready for the Turning Point; Growers; Jumpstarters; True Stewards.

Sector II: Administrators; Procedure Managers; Clerkoids; Monitors; Motivators; Policemen; Straw Bosses; Fear Managers.

Sector III: Organizational Parasites; Dead Batteries; Indulgers; Secret-Keepers; Fear Victims.

Sector IV: Indulgees; Observers; Hi Touch–No Tech; Pop-wisdom Seekers; Followers.

sure, but I am also sure that the old control/command model of management *pushed* many managers and employees into this attitude of disengagement.

The folks in Sector II are those described in several books as being more concerned about doing things right than about doing the right things. If they can let go of that need to "fill in the boxes" and can redirect some of their legitimate caring by understanding that, in order to really care for the organization, they must also care for the people (which oftentimes means redefining the word *mistake*), they may have the capacity to move into Sector I.

I worry most about the people in Sector IV. Their professed caring about others while not caring so much about the organization just does not ring true. Further, it perpetuates the old dualism about the separateness of relationships and work. It's like saying to one's fellow employees, "I care about you, but I don't care about what you do." Just try saying that to a colleague sometime.

As for me, I'm glad Ken Mishoe cared enough about me to share this handy visual aid.

He ended his note with this: "I think you still owe me a lunch."

And I think I *still* do. But not for long.

Beware the Big Happy Family

I find many people attracted to the idea of "family" as a model for work relationships, but I tell managers that, in their quest to create the right kind of working environment, they should resist the temptation to ever say, "We're just one big happy family around here."

It's one thing for people who work together to develop, over time, a connection and feeling somewhat like that of family; it's quite another thing for the manager to see the employee group as a family, for it can also mean that the boss sees himself or herself as the parent.

I talk a lot about the command/control model of organization as the source of much dysfunction in the workplace, but it could just be that the "big parent" model of management has caused every bit as much organizational dysfunction, and may even be more difficult to change.

That's because there are two groups that probably feel very comfortable with the idea of a big parent running the operation: bosses and, yes, employees.

And why wouldn't both groups be comfortable? History—even the Bible—is full of this way of relating between the "boss" (king, queen, emperor, pharaoh, God) and the "employees" (the people). In fact, the whole notion of the omnipotent parent who can be benign on the one hand and judgmental and punishing on the other is deeply rooted in all of us.

We are comfortable with that image, so much so that when we are acting as the parent/boss, we even feel *spiritually justified* in our behavior, benign or judgmental; and when we are the employee/people, we *accept* those actions as being spiritually justified. After all, we've been told all our lives that God works in mysterious ways and many things just are not to be revealed to us. We've been conditioned to know that parents have to do things for our own good, even though we may not understand them at the time.

I think that's why many employees will allow their own feelings of worth to rise or fall on the sometimes mercurial opinions of the boss.

I worked once with a bright and talented man who was decent and sensitive to his colleagues at all levels. We shared the same boss, a man whose rare compliments and praise were, in my opinion, far outweighed by his frequent harsh judgments.

I saw this boss, who was at least six years younger than my sensitive friend, insult and humiliate my friend on several occasions—yet my friend seemed to live just for the boss's rare compliments, which, incidentally, I always felt were contrived and insincere.

"Why," I asked him one day, "can you put up with all that verbal abuse, then become so fawningly appreciative when he gives you a long-overdue compliment?"

My friend explained: "Because he is so judgmental and critical, it makes the compliments all the more valuable."

"Kinda like, keep on beating me because it feels so good when you stop?"

My friend just laughed.

But I was serious, because it is this distorted way of expressing positive comments (compliments, love, appreciation) that has screwed up so many family relationships and undermined the self-esteem of so many people.

Once again, there are plenty of historical—yes, including biblical—examples of the harsh parent God putting the children (people) through all manner of torment and hardship in the name of love, then showering them with blessings to prove *his* love even though, it should be understood, they are not truly worthy of that love.

Wait. I fully understand that in the interest of offering the *superficial* biblical example, I risk trivializing the deeper theological messages. That is not my intent, nor am I offering a comment one way or another about religious beliefs: I wish only to emphasize that we are very comfortable with this model of a righteous authority figure, and it is just as difficult for the employees to change as it is for the bosses to change.

And I know this: The change must begin with the managers. They must begin to think of the workplace as a community in which everybody has equal worth and dignity as human beings, regardless of whether or not each job has equal value to the business enterprise.

That's why I consider it important to pay attention to the vocabulary used to refer to the workplace, and why I consider it a danger signal when managers call their companies or departments or work groups "a big happy family."

Chances are it ain't so.

Thinking for Number Four

I was talking with an old air force pilot buddy the other day and he reminded me of another definition of leadership. It's called "thinking for number four." And it's perfect.

Jet fighters often fly in formations of four planes, with number one being the leader. The leader has a very heavy responsibility, literally a responsibility of life and death. Everyone in the flight depends on the leader.

There was a newspaper story a few years ago—unfortunately, there have been several of them over the years—in which a flight of four jets in an aerobatics demonstration team crashed in perfect formation, killing all four pilots. Some people are surprised by these stories because they don't understand that the pilots of planes number two, three, and four are flying the leader's wing and will follow the leader anywhere, *even into the ground.*

This is not a matter of blind obedience; it is simply that the leader is the one who should have the most accurate picture of where the flight is going.

The analogy applies very well to business. Even though the leader should always be sharing the vision and empowering people to act on that vision, the leader still must be sensitive to the risks for everyone and must be careful not to lead the enterprise into jeopardy.

In other words, the leader has to think constantly for number four.

Everybody's Talkin'
About Quality, Too

Two of the subjects I am asked about most frequently these days are "continuous improvement" and/or "total quality management" (TQM). I like to say that these concepts basically are not about quality, and they're not about management—except as they are subsets of something else: relationships.

I believe that at least half of the CEOs who sign on for TQM initially expect it to be a process of "getting more quality out of the employees," by establishing systems of monitoring and measurement. They usually are not prepared for the *revolution* in social architecture, in culture, in interpersonal relationships that must occur for TQM to fully flower into top-quality results for the company.

But I am no expert on TQM, so my answers usually begin with the question: Just what *does* "quality" really mean?

Quality has something in common with ethics in that many people in business want to define both quality and ethics in terms that won't get in the way of "doing business."

That's because both quality and ethics get a little messy when we try to apply them to what we do in business every day and to what the marketplace sometimes seems to be pushing us incessantly to do.

Leaving ethics for another day, let me talk a bit about quality. No easy task, since quality, like beauty, is often in the eye of the beholder, and in business in the past couple of decades, the "beholder" frequently has been a "numbers person" who sees quality in a product only in terms of its cost, not its benefits. In those cases, the definition of "good quality" is likely to change for the worse, and the product is likely to suffer.

Often the attack on quality is not made directly, but is masked in code, such as:

"We have to be the low-cost producer."

"We *can* cut costs without cutting quality."

"I've seen no research that proves the consumers notice a thinner grade of metal (or plastic or paper or whatever the case may be)."

And that old favorite we learned as children: "All the other companies are doing it."

The hard reality is that there usually is some truth to these arguments. Sometimes, in fact, the savings represented by these cuts in quality have meant the difference between survival and going out of business.

But none of this really gets to what I believe is the heart of the matter, because quality, like ethics, transcends the most obvious definitions.

A definition of good quality surely must include the quality of the product, which begins with a good concept, design, and a strong reason for being, which then is translated into a positive message of benefit for the potential customer.

And it also must include the technical quality, which means simply that it must perform for the customer.

But there's another part of the definition: the quality of relationships—between managers and employees, between the employees and the customers, between the owners (stockholders) and the management, between the company and its suppliers, and between the company and the community at large.

It is interesting that when we talk about quality in business, we most always talk about quality of the product itself; yet most of the press coverage of any industry, in the trades as well as in the consumer press, is about the quality of *relationships,* and most often about failed or failing relationships.

The cost of quality clearly cuts both ways; businesses can spend more than it's worth, and businesses can cost-cut themselves into serious trouble. Managing quality is indeed a gigantic balancing act, but I believe we spend far too much time and effort examining only the costs of good or bad product quality and not enough examining the costs of good or bad relationships.

The companies that concentrate on the relationships are the ones most likely to achieve quality in everything they do.

(And politicians, elected officials, educators, religious leaders, and others take note: This is true of all other communities, as well.)

Business's Bum Rap

Dear Sue:

I was distressed by our quick conversation about the excesses of business. I don't want to be an apologist for those things that truly are excesses, but I contend that business has taken a bum rap.

To begin, business is not monolithic. There is no one business voice or business attitude or business opinion. Oh, there are groups which, to one extent or another, attempt to speak for "business," but not one of them authentically does it. In fact, no one group speaks for even the majority of business.

Just as I contend that there are no business ethics, only people ethics, I contend also that there are no business attitudes or opinions, only attitudes or opinions of people in business. And those vary not only between industries and between companies, but also *within* companies.

Next, business changes. No institution changes more dramatically when the need for change is perceived. Why? Because there is an incentive to change.

As you know, I used to prefer government "solutions" to business "solutions." I used to think, "At least I have a vote in government; I have no vote in business."

I was wrong. My vote in government seems to diminish while, as business becomes more competitive, my vote as a customer (that is, the money I can spend) becomes more important and more sought after.

Of course, I still feel government must regulate certain practices and must have an important role in assuring fair dealing in business and in assuring social justice. What has changed is my opinion about the respective roles of government and business in bringing about a more equitable society.

It's a damned shame that money for political campaigns has become the dominant influence in the public policy arena. Everyone knows what to do about it, but there are no incentives to do it. The situation gets no better.

In business, just as there are incentives to change, there are disincentives not to change. Thus, business is becoming much more responsive to the human needs of its employees and to its customers. There is much talk of being responsive and responsible to all "stakeholders."

Why? Because it's the right thing to do? Only partly, and only among the most leading-edge leaders and their companies. Mostly, it's because it's the smart business thing to do.

In the quest for good people to fill all the information, service, and knowledge jobs to be created by the turn of the century, companies must accommodate an increasingly diverse work force: people of all racial and ethnic backgrounds, people in all kinds of family arrangements, older people who twenty years ago would be retired, people with disabilities, and on and on.

So not only do I think business gets a bum rap, I think business can be at the forefront of social change. That's what I meant when I told you that I am ready to give businesspeople incentives to bring this free-enterprise, entrepreneurial, problem-solving approach to some of our seemingly intransigent social-justice problems.

This isn't a new idea, of course, but it does seem to me that the time has come to stop condemning business people for all of capitalism's deficiencies without recognizing its contributions and its potential. And it is time for more understanding about the role of government tax policies in providing incentives or disincentives (often erroneously called "loopholes" by the critics) for businesses to engage in certain kinds of activities.

With that understanding, we should then start giving incentives for business to take on some of those things that have proved difficult and frequently ineffective for the government to do.

On the other hand, there are still those excesses we need to "disincent" business from doing. But I'll save that subject for another day. Meanwhile, my sweet, do your uncle Jim a favor and start looking for some of the good things businesses are doing for society. You might be surprised.

With love,
Your grouchy businessman uncle

Diagnosing the "Yeah, Buts"

Let's face it. A lot of top business people are sourasses.

It would be funny if it weren't so sad. After all, work contains every emotion of life—or is supposed to—which means that we should experience a lot of joy and celebration from our work, not to mention personal growth and fulfillment.

So why is it that so many management people, successful by any common business-school standard, seem not to feel comfortable unless they also feel worried?

Even if business is good and morale is good and all the numbers are good and the owners (stockholders) are happy, the top people never seem to celebrate.

They frown. They harrumph. And they break out in a bad case of the "YEAH, BUTS."

"Hey, boss," you say, "our plan is on target. Sales are good. New product development is coming along. Profits are at an all-time high."

And the boss says: "YEAH, BUT what will these interest rates do to things next year?"

"Won't matter," you say, "things are so solid that these rates can only help."

At this point, you're waiting for the smile, the congratulations, the thumbs-up sign.

And then the boss is attacked by a malady that is a frequent side effect of the YEAH, BUTS: The "YEAH, BUT WHAT IFS."

So the boss says, "YEAH, BUT WHAT IF the Congress passes another regulation, the president fails to veto it, another volcano erupts in the Philippines, there's an earthquake in our biggest market area, our competitors undercut our prices by 50 percent, and the nations of the former Soviet Union get back together and attack Germany?"

At this point, you realize that your proper demeanor is one of worry, so you say, "Yeah, boss, that's a worry, all right. We'll keep an eye on all that."

Only then might the boss seem relaxed.

It's no mystery to me why so many of these guys (and I do mean guys) seem to wither up and die after they retire. They just don't have enough to worry about.

Everybody's Doin' It

Watching some of the machinations top executives are putting their people and their companies through these days, I get to wondering how many business leaders really know what to do—or even think they do.

It's becoming like some sort of follow-the-leader game, except that only a few of them seem to understand what the real leaders are doing. The media report that big company X is reorganizing or "flattening the organization" or "downsizing" (excuse me, that's "rightsizing") or "reengineering" for "time-based competitiveness" or turning themselves into "learning organizations." Or they are changing their "architecture" in order to create work groups organized around "process" rather than "function"—requiring, of course, that the work groups be "empowered."

Once the business media report these activities, it seems that companies begin to jump on the bandwagon. Company Y, then Company Z, then A, B, and C. Pretty soon, the whole alphabet is in turmoil.

I don't put the above activities in quotes because I criticize them as concepts, or don't believe they work. To the contrary, I know that we live in a changing world, and I fervently believe that the philosophical, conceptual, and organizational frameworks in which business operates must change, too, and I think many of these new concepts are wonderful and have the capacity to move American business forward in very significant ways.

What bugs me is that some business executives are just

playing follow the leader, or follow the current management fad, whether their companies need it or not. Their actions are more a matter of ego than of thoughtful management.

The process of deciding what to do must start with the stakeholders: customers, owners, employees, vendors, community at large. What is the business purpose of embracing a particular change?

I submit that even the best of these concepts and systems will not work for every kind of business—yet, as American corporations have come in the past years to the age of the professional manager, there has been an accompanying belief that the good manager can manage any kind of company, that the good leader can be effective in any environment. This has brought an assumption that whatever organizational structures, systems, concepts, and so on are good for one company are good for all companies.

This just is not true; not only between companies but even within companies, it is not true.

Furthermore, the execution of any concept or practice makes a huge difference. Take total quality management (hereinafter referred to as TQM). There probably is no more dramatic example of how something gets screwed up than TQM. According to MIT professor Peter Senge author of *The Fifth Discipline,* even Dr. Edwards Deming, originator of TQM, disavows the ways many companies have tried to turn TQM into a quick fix-it system in which people are pressured to perform good quality rather than manifest TQM as an essential and fundamental change in the workplace's social architecture or culture.

Trying to fit TQM into the old control/command model of management—with which so many managers are comfortable—is a complete distortion of TQM. With TQM, and with most of the new concepts I alluded to, people within an organization have to change their thinking and their entire conceptual framework.

But this is not the way many top executives want to change. Yes, they recognize the necessity of change (and if they didn't recognize it, they'd be ashamed to say so, because change is now so much a part of the conventional wisdom.) So they want to change, but not all that much. This means they try to change as little as possible, which leads them sometimes to try to fit the new concept into the old environment, or to try to do just a piece of the new concept. Many of them have tried that with TQM.

And look also at what has happened with "downsizing" (excuse me, "rightsizing"). Of course, some layoffs and restructurings have been necessary and important. But there has also been a lot of self-defeating nonsense going on. Many companies set arbitrary percentages for cutting their work forces, and they laid off a lot of people, many of whom were middle managers. It was, as you know, a massive white-collar layoff, unprecedented, in fact.

The idea, of course, was to flatten the organization, to get rid of redundant layers of management. Sounded good, but somewhere along the way, many of those top executives seemed to forget what the middle managers were doing in the first place. Most senior managers thought the middle managers were "processing information." This led to the belief that, with technology making the information processing function easier, middle managers were not necessary after all.

But there was another function middle managers were fulfilling: that of representing top management to the workers and representing the workers to top management, of counseling, of leading the team. Put another way, the middle managers were often buffers and chaplains.

The top executives also overlooked the fact that if organizations are truly to be "flattened," then the top people must let go of their need to be "in control," to be "on top of everything." This meant they had to take themselves out of much of the decision-making, which in turn meant that there would be decisions made and executed *before they even knew about them.* If you are one of those managers who defines being "on top of the business" as knowing everything that's going on at a given time, then this kind of "empowerment" of people to make their own decisions is very threatening.

And yet, this letting go of control is at the very essence of flattening an organization, of empowering the people and the work groups, of putting decision-making at the lowest level of competency. Without closing that part of the loop, the laying off and "flattening" was just symbolic; in other words, a sham. And for many companies, as Peter Drucker pointed out in his book *Managing for the Future,* the overhead they thought they were saving by laying off people just came back. It came back because they had tried to take an important concept and simply execute the most obvious and publicly dramatic part of it.

And I believe that some of those actions were taken because some CEOs just had the impression that all the big-time companies and executives were doing it, so it must be a good thing to do. Unfortunately, it may be years before the full effect of those cutbacks is felt, and for many companies, they will be felt in a lack of new products coming on line or in a degradation of customer service or in a decline in product quality.

Only then will some of these executives discover that they weren't following the real leaders after all; they were following the followers.

DOWNSIZING

Too many times has a death message
come late at night
for me not to fill with fear
when the telephone pulls me awake.

And when I hear the voice,
I know the news is bad.
"How can they just eliminate my job like that?"
I don't know.
"After all these years?"
I don't know.

We talk a long time
about when we were younger
and everything was uncertain
but full of promise,
thinking then that money was the goal
and the job was just something we did.

But now we know the truth.
"I can get by financially, I guess,
but that's not the point.
It's the work."
"Yes."

Then at this pause,
from the silence on the end of the phone,
comes at last that same sound

of other late-night phone calls,
grief, loss, disconnection,
and yet something else,
something like rejection,
but even more than that,
as if a whole life of work
has been without worth,
so insignificant that it can be legislated away,
the way some governments
simply erase all traces
of a person's life and work,
as if he had never existed.

The phone fills with silence.
Finally, as after those other death messages,
there is nothing left to say
except the trivial.
My old colleague apologizes for waking me
and trusts that I won't be tired in the morning
and fears I have been upset
and knows there is nothing I can do
and hopes we can get together soon
and appreciates my support
and may call me for a reference
and wishes my family well.

DEATH MESSAGE

I was in the big strategic planning meeting,
of all places,
the once a year pull out all the stops
and try to convince everyone including ourselves
that we know what tomorrow will bring
and if it brings something different
we will be ready meeting,
when my secretary, eyes down and head shaking,
handed me the note:
"They want you at the hospital . . . Red's failing fast."

It does not work to say
that we are all dying
and it is simply a question of when;
it does not make death more natural
nor does it make us less surprised
even when we are expecting it.

"Any day now," we had been saying,
yet it seemed to me Red's last prank,
dying in the middle
of a strategic planning meeting,
knowing I would pick up and leave
and the planning department's beautiful schedule
would be forever out of whack
because death is just not a contingency
they know how to plan for.

His lung had collapsed by the time I arrived
but over the respirator mask
his eyes widened and he squeezed my hand
with more strength than he could spare.
His brother-in-law said,
"Hell, he's gone, he's not here now"
even though the breathing had not stopped.
And I thought of meetings and trips and parties,
of where he started and how far he came
from a tiny town in Iowa to a big publishing company
and how much he brought with him,
old-fashioned stuff and corny as hell,
yet something we all came to depend on
and would never be able to replace.

The next morning on my desk,
another note from my secretary:
"They finished the meeting without you."
And I thought,
it won't be the last time.

OBSOLETE

"I just can't talk to them anymore.
They're kids, they don't listen."
It was the last thing he could say,
all that remained from a life of selling
which stretched from a smile and a shine
to a couple of martinis,
a flip chart,
and enough orders to send the kids to college.
It's the face you sell, he had thought,
shaving each morning,
and he could always go out and sell it
to anybody regardless of the product.
And he knew he'd never lose his gift of gab,
from his mother's Irish side,
but it never crossed his mind
that just when things ought to ease off,
when he should be able
to coast on into retirement,
he would find himself among people
who thought everything he said
sounded like some lost language,
quaint but without meaning for them.

DEBTS AND PAYMENTS

World War II was mostly movies to me,
certainly not headlines,
because I did not read the papers then.
Even the war news came as newsreels
in the movie houses,
so the planes and tanks and soldiers
all were bigger than life,
heroic beyond my imagination,
and we would rush home and play war
shooting and pretending we were hit,
contorting our faces in agony
but always managing to toss one last grenade,
littering our neighborhood with dead nazis and japs.
After the war soldiers returned
with medals and money and war brides.
And stories.
Slowly we learned that the storytellers
had not seen much combat
and that the quiet ones had the real stories
but they were not telling.

Years later, in the 1980s, I worked with a man,
short, a bit pudgy, quiet,
a man of modest ambition
who did a mechanical job competently
but with obvious reluctance to even be noticed
much less be promoted into more responsibility.
He was in my operating group,

which means I was his big boss,
and in reviewing a staffing plan,
I was told it was not he who was judged extraneous
to the new way of doing things,
it was his job.
I was about to okay the plan
when the quiet man's supervisor
said, "This is not exactly relevant,
but I wasn't sure you knew
that he commanded one of the first tanks to reach
the Rhine . . . saw a lot of action."

No, it was not relevant
to our new way of doing things,
but I could think only of what pain,
what real contortion of face and body,
what smells and sounds,
what fear
he must have witnessed
while I was playing war in the grass.

"We'll wait," I said, to reactions
clearly divided by generations.
"Some things just cost a little extra."
Other things are never fully paid.

Management as an Act of Faith

I always support management decisions to bring in outside help to do motivational workshops for the people. From time to time, any group seems to need a shot in the arm from another source, and you, the manager, will benefit as well. The people need to hear the same things said in different ways, and you need to hear other vocabularies, which you might be able to adopt.

It is just good leadership to be constantly seeking different ways of saying the same thing in order to be sure you, as a manager, are communicating effectively to everyone in your department. At the same time, never lose sight of the one thing you need to keep yourself going and to keep your people going:

Faith.

Oops! That's a word I've not used before in the business context—but in fact, I have used thousands of words to convey the concept of faith.

Remember *Damn Yankees*? If so, you remember the song, "You Gotta Have Heart," which the baseball manager sings to his team.

Not only is it, in today's terms, an old song, but its message is far older than the song itself. One of the first places we may remember hearing that message was in *The Little Engine That Could*. If I were a scholar, I could begin at the earliest of recorded history and, working my way through the literature and the religious writings of all civilization, find this message in thousands of forms.

One of the things to learn about messages (and even

clichés) that endure for many years is that there must be some important truth in there somewhere.

I think the important truth of faith has to do with its power not only to motivate us and keep us focused, but also its own self-fulfilling power to make things happen.

We seem reluctant to use the vocabularies of our religions to apply to our businesses, yet if the lessons of those religions apply to our lives, they must apply to our businesses.

What, for instance, does the entrepreneur bring besides a good idea, energy, and the willingness to take risks? According to the experts I know, the entrepreneur never loses his or her focus on the potential outcome. The entrepreneur seems, even at the most discouraging points, to "see" an image, to envision what the successful business will look like. I'd call that faith.

I used to work with a magazine advertising director who felt he could sell anything. I made a call with him one time on what I felt was a most unlikely account. The senior vice president of this company took my friend to task for even making the call.

"It takes a wild imagination to think our product belongs in your magazine," the senior VP said. "You're wasting my time."

My friend kept selling. "Please, Mr. B———," the executive said, "I'm asking you nicely to just leave my office now."

Embarrassed, I stood up, loaded my briefcase, but almost had to pull my friend physically toward the door.

"Yes, sir, I do respect your time and I'm sorry that you

feel I've wasted it, so I'll do as you ask and leave now," said my friend.

"Thank you," said the senior VP.

At the door, my friend paused, looked back and said, "But I'll be calling to see if we can set up another meeting. I think I still have a few points you'll find compelling."

I'm sure I gasped out loud, but the senior VP just shook his head and laughed. "You're a helluva salesman," he said.

We left. I said, "My God, I thought he was going to call security. You pushed pretty hard."

"I know," said my friend. Then he smiled, "But he didn't say no."

Pure, raw faith.

We know business runs in cycles and we know that during down periods, the best among us keep trying different ideas and new approaches rather than just waiting for the cycle to turn. I call that faith.

I've seen many renewals and new beginnings, of companies, of products, of people. At those times, I am struck by an underlying hope of the new, the sense that we can make things better.

I feel there are lessons in all of this for business, and I find myself asking questions like, "Even in business, aren't we supposed to try to be messiahs for one another? Isn't it perhaps possible to think of ourselves as messiahs for our products?

"Haven't we seen people whose lives seemed almost destroyed by marital problems or substance abuse return to a full and productive life? Couldn't that be called a resurrection? Is it going too far to say that when we save a dying product, we have resurrected it—and mean it as a spiritual endeavor rather than just as a phrase?"

So especially in business these days do I think we gotta have heart and vision and commitment and a can-do attitude—all those things that perhaps add up to faith.

In closing, consider the business implications of this quote from Saint Augustine: "Faith is to believe that which you cannot see; the reward of faith is to see that which you did not believe."

The Definition of Insanity

Members of the press raised their collective eyebrows last year about then newly elected Vice President Al Gore's vocabulary. They noted, in almost accusatory tones, that Vice President Gore was "using the language of recovery groups."

To the reporters' way of thinking, he was doing it in order to woo the votes of all those people who are, or have been, involved in twelve-step groups of one sort or another: Alcoholics Anonymous, substance-abuse groups, compulsive-eating-disorder groups, stop-smoking groups, and so on.

I disagree. I think the vice president was tapping into an understanding that participants in these "recovery groups" know is basic to overcoming their problems, and I believe he was suggesting that the country must come to this same understanding. Let me add that I believe businesspeople most especially must come to this understanding.

To paraphrase the "Big Book" of Alcoholics Anonymous, the definition of *insanity* is doing the same thing over and over again, but expecting a different result.

Larry Wilson, at the Pecos River Conference Center, puts it in a more rhythmical way: "If you keep on doing what you've always done, you'll keep on getting what you've always got."

So, we might ask, why are so many companies so preoccupied with doing the same old thing, insanely expecting a different result?

There are two answers, I believe. One is that the people running those companies made their reputations and rose up through the organization on the basis of doing the same thing and getting the same result for years and years. It is understandable that they would resist change. The difference, of course, is that businesses these days need a different result.

The second answer has to do with some high-level expectation that the results will yield to tinkering or to imposing quick-fix ideas onto the organization without fundamental change from top to bottom. This, in fact, has been the root cause of the failure of many ideas that otherwise could have made positive changes.

In the quest for a fix, I have seen top managers bring in consultants to introduce a new system (TQM comes to mind), thinking that the system itself will change the results without the managers themselves having to change at all.

In fact, these managers will change organization structure, systems, employees—anything at all *except* themselves. Then they wonder why the fix hasn't worked.

Their attitude is supremely arrogant, without self-awareness or introspection or humility (the very characteristics, incidentally, that twelve-step groups help people develop in themselves). This compulsion against change and growth has led, and is leading, good companies—some of them very large and very prestigious—down a ruinous road.

And that is, for the lack of a better word, insane.

We're Here to Work

Dear Art:

Perhaps the most destructive delusion in which we humans collectively engage is the notion that our lives will become happier, richer, and fuller once we don't have to work anymore. Connected to that, of course, is the belief that if we could suddenly strike it rich, we'd quit our jobs (telling the boss to "take this job and shove it" is always part of the fantasy), and live the good life. The classic dream these days is winning the lottery.

Rarely is anyone given the chance to realize that the good life is not so good without the growth and fulfillment that work most often provides, whether you need the income or not.

Now comes a wonderful case in point. In the *Des Moines Register* on Monday, September 7, 1992, there was a report about Mr. Bill Watson, who won four million dollars in the Iowa lottery in 1985.

Naturally, the first thing he did was quit his job as a firefighter. Why not? He was to receive an after-tax check for $150,037.50 a year every year through 2004. Why work? We work for money, right?

Wrong, so Bill Watson discovered.

As of 1992, though he owned six cars and took regular vacations, was single, and had what by any popular measurement would be the good life, he applied for his job back at the firehouse.

"We're all put on earth to work, not just to exist," he explained, and he missed his job. He missed it all: having to get up at a certain time, reporting in, the camaraderie of the workplace, even looking forward to a day off.

What Bill Watson discovered is that he *loved* his job.

Just think of the dedication he would take with him to his old job now that he has made that most fundamental of discoveries about those things we set ourselves to do in this life, our work, however that is defined.

From the conversations you and I have had about the importance of work, you know how strongly I feel that managers must make more effort to recognize and honor this elementary need of people, and must work to create a workplace in which that need can be met, in which people can actually engage their work in a way that ennobles them and brings meaning to their efforts.

Instead, most managers and their companies also affirm the myth that people dislike working and, given the chance, would walk away from it. By assuming that people really don't want to work, we establish rules and policies and procedures that serve to restrict rather than enable or empower people.

Fortunately, there are those managers who recognize that the greatest reward they can provide for their employees is to do everything possible to make the work itself meaningful.

Or to understand, in Bill Watson's wise words, "If you don't work, it just takes a lot of enjoyment out of life."

Well put. In other words, if you win the lottery, don't quit your job.

Love,
Dad

A LONG WAY TO DRIVE

Some days I wish I had
a jug of coffee and a long way to drive,
down some blacktop
in the middle of nowhere,
headed to somewhere
but in no hurry.
When the tank moved toward empty,
I'd stop,
or when my eyes fell on some smoky shack
with a pile of hickory wood outside
and an RC COLA sign
with BAR-B-Q on it,
I'd pull in,
and when my dust cloud settled,
I'd decide on beans or slaw,
and that would be it,
my big decision of the day.

But I hear somewhere in the back of my head
a country boy saying, "Horseshit,
anybody believe that, take out a eyeball."
I hear him talking about how
I used to drive blacktop roads,
moaning every mile of the way
about making a lot of money some day
and working in an office
and traveling anywhere
and having a big car

and knowing a lot of important people.
"In the high cotton," I'd say,
"up among the high rafter bats."

Everything they ever said was true
about what money can't buy,
but they never said it's easier
to believe what money can't buy
after you have some money
you can't buy it with.

Understanding Worth
and Value

Dear Clare:

It is testimony to your decency that you have doubts and difficulty in aligning in your own mind the relationships between people and their compensation. I completely understand your reactions to the fact that some of your nicest, most enthusiastic team members are not as well paid as others who are not so likable. And I know it is tough when some of those nice people ask why.

I think it is particularly challenging for managers as well as employees to come to grips with the issue of worth versus value in the workplace. No, I don't mean pricing the product, I mean the application of those terms to the people themselves.

We all are so driven by our desire to make the connection between what we are paid and what we are worth that we tend to let far too much of our self-esteem and the perception of others' opinions of us ride on the symbols of our "worth" in the marketplace. We live in certain neighborhoods or drive certain kinds of cars, take vacations to certain places, and so on.

Social critics may decry what they call conspicuous consumption or blatant materialism or, put another way, keeping up with the Joneses, but the reality is that in our search for inner feelings about worth, we want also to let others know how our worth has paid off in the world of commerce. So we buy stuff.

The amount of stuff we buy depends on the amount of money we have (or our credit rating), and the amount of money we have depends usually on our salaries or wages.

So it is always hard to swallow that someone else, a colleague or peer, is paid more than we are.

"Why," someone may ask, "should Shirley in New York sales be paid more than I am? My job as a direct-marketing salesperson is as important as hers."

What that person is really saying, I believe, is that the "company believes that Shirley is 'worth' more that I am."

What has happened is exactly what I have often warned managers and their employees about: the confusion of worth of the person and value of the job.

It's another management paradox.

In managing people over the years, I always proceeded with the assumption that every person in my care as a manager had basic human worth, deserved dignity and fair treatment, and should be respected as a human being.

On the other hand, I also knew that *jobs* had different values to the enterprise. So while all people may be equal in their worth as human beings and members of the community of work, and while everyone's voice should be listened to and heard in the management of the business, *not every job is of equal value.* Factors like education, training, experience, tenure, market competition (supply and demand within the professional field or a geographic area) must be powerful determinants in setting salary and wage scales.

I was always straight with employees about this, although I knew many of them still felt there were issues of equity and fairness in making these determinations. Nonetheless, I felt it vital to make a clear distinction between worth of the individual and value of the job.

Not to do so, in my observation, has led many managers to judge people's worth by the importance of the job. In other words, the people in the more "valuable" jobs (usually revenue-producing jobs versus support and administrative jobs) are regarded as more valuable people—thus connecting money to human worth. The most blatant public display of this came in Leona Helmsley's alleged comments about the "little people," meaning, of course, those without wealth.

I have never seen the evaluation made the other way around. I have never seen the manager who said, "Well, he is such a worthwhile person that I now consider that particular job to be of more value to the enterprise."

Neither approach would be correct, of course. Open and honest explanation is your only tool in confronting this paradox—that, and a redoubling of your day-to-day efforts to assure that all employees can find meaning and dignity and fulfillment in their jobs, which is the real worth of work.

With love,
Dad

Assuring the Future of Capitalism

Now that capitalism has "won" the great world struggle, and communism, despite a few rebounds by hard-liners here and there, seems the one doomed to the ash heap of history, it's time to take a look at prospects for the winner.

I have no doubt that the future of capitalism is brighter than ever. It is here to stay. It clearly has demonstrated itself to be a superior economic system and one that has the capacity to perform for the greater social good.

And yet, just as we face this bright future, we must also recognize that within capitalism are the seeds of its own destruction.

Much depends on definition. If we define capitalism as the application of capital (which of course includes many resources beyond money) to the doing of commerce—the making and moving and buying and selling of goods and services—with the intention of returning for the investors (the "capitalists") a *fair return* on their investment (this includes "earnings," or cash flow, return on equity, return on investment, and other measurements), then I think capitalism has a bright future.

If, on the other hand, we define capitalism in the same way, *but* restate the intention as *not* being a "fair return" but instead, being one of "unrestrained pursuit of profit and increased owner value by doing whatever it takes," then capitalism is headed for trouble.

I have just returned from a forum on business in which

a distinguished business school professor said that we cannot return to a nostalgic fifties' view of business in which people can expect to have long-term employment. Instead, businesses have to remain flexible so they can eliminate jobs or change their geographic location. This professor then said that the new responsibility of business is to make people "employable," but not let them expect long-term employment.

There was a good deal of applause on this point. However, that same professor had just told the group that in order for businesses to grow and prosper, the leaders were to embrace innovations from the grass roots and were to reward mistakes and were to share power with people at the lowest levels of the organization. ("Empowerment." We're hearing that one a lot lately.)

Well, I'm no scholar, but I have been a manager for thirty years, and I believe that if businesses are so "flexible" they are regularly giving signals to people that jobs may be eliminated, operations moved to other states or countries, and so on, then those businesses have lost sight of some fairly basic truths. Among them are:

1. The people at the grass roots are not going to innovate and come up with new ideas for products and processes if they're worried about their jobs. They won't feel they owe this to the company, and they'll be scared to do anything new.

2. The people will not trust that the company will reward their mistakes. "Big talk," they'll say (and if history is a teacher, they'll probably be right).

3. The people will not accept all that "empowerment"

because—need I say it again?—they'll simply be scared of doing something they've not been told to do.

4. Companies will find themselves facing sort of a new kind of labor movement—only this time, in addition to organizing into bargaining units, individual workers will pursue their claims of "job as property right" in the courts.

Also bearing on the concept of "unrestrained pursuit of profit" is the question of responsibility to the society at large. This includes issues of poverty, race, gender, health care, and the environment.

We have for a long time been in this dynamic tension between those theorists who believe that a business's only social responsibility is to pursue profit, which in turn makes jobs and contributes to the greater social good; and those theorists who believe that business exists within a complex economic, political, social, and educational ecosystem to which business must be sensitive, responsive, and contributive in a direct way.

Count me among the latter theorists, but not on the basis of theory, on the basis of common sense.

As I have traveled recently—consulting, speaking, and conducting workshops—I have sensed a wave sweeping across business in America. It is a wave of *positive intent*, of good values, of community. It is called by many names, but it is my most fervent hope that this "movement" will play itself out into what I call Enlightened Capitalism.

If this happens, as I believe it will, then capitalism has a bright future indeed.

Making a Whole Partnership

Business has been full of talk in the past several years about alliances and joint ventures and partnerships. Many business observers suggest that these kinds of arrangements may be the best way for American businesses to expand globally.

Some talk of a new era of "partnering." They say that companies are abandoning old notions of being conglomerates, of owning many different businesses or entering many different lines of business. Instead, they are establishing partnerships to make these entries; in other words, they are settling for only half the pie and, in doing so, are taking only half the risk.

Why, we may wonder, is this emphasis on partnering gaining such momentum? Some point to the *keiretsu* of the Japanese, to the various European consortia, and to other models.

Whatever it's called, it gets down to working together in order to accomplish a mutually defined and mutually desirable goal, usually market position and/or profits.

It is easier said than done, however. I have some experiences with strategic alliances as well as partnerships, and I can assure you that it's easy to get all caught up in the wonderful results we'll be able to achieve together, without sufficiently examining and planning for the human dimensions involved in working together in the first place. There's the rub. And it should be no surprise.

The concept of partnership has undergone some

daunting challenges in the past decade or so in this country. I believe that often, we in business, or in the educational community, in the religious community, in the political community, even in our own personal relationships, have moved away from a traditional concept of partnership.

Often we have not asked the old question—What can I give to this partnership?—but have substituted the new question, the question of the past decade—What can I get from this partnership?

I think the fundamental reason to create a partnership *should never change,* and that is the belief that by working together, sharing the risk, sharing the reward, *and* sharing creativity, innovation, and energy, the individual partners will have more success than if they tried it alone. It's that overused word of the seventies, *synergy.*

This fundamental reason for partnering works properly only if it rests on another fundamental belief that has been expressed in many ways but which I boil down to the golden rule: Do unto your partner as you would have your partner do unto you.

Does that sound too high-minded, too soft and mushy? I assure you that while it may be high-minded (strange that we are expected these days to have to justify high-mindedness, isn't it?), it is not soft and mushy. It is, in fact, a difficult and demanding discipline, a rigorous standard, and an unrelenting challenge.

But it is also the key to success in any kind of partnership.

For the question truly is How can I make sure that my partner is getting as much from this as I am? and not

How can I make sure I get my share? (which, translated, usually means more than my partner gets).

So in considering partnership, I ask my business colleagues and clients also to consider these thoughts about giving, rather than receiving.

That's the way to create what I call a whole partnership.

An Admittedly Defensive Letter About Executive Pay

Dear Sue:

You raise a good question about executive pay, and I can understand your feelings of anger about it.

Surely, in a world in which people are starving, and in a country in which people are without homes, it seems grossly unfair on the face of it that some people should be paid several million dollars a year for simply working at a job, no matter how "big" the job is perceived to be.

I appreciate also that you challenged what I wrote in *Love and Profit* about favoring "competitive executive pay in keeping with the responsibilities and risks of the job."

Let me tell you what I mean by that, and let me tell you how I think compensation, not just executive pay, should work.

To begin, I do not believe in some sort of arbitrary way of determining executive pay. The most popular formula now seems to be a multiple of the workers' pay, expressed as, "The CEO should be paid twenty times the average of the salaries of all workers in the company," or "The CEO should be paid twenty times the average salary of the lowest-paid workers in the company."

My response to that is, "Should we then assure that each employee is carrying one-twentieth the responsibility of the CEO, or that the average employee's job carries one-twentieth the risk of the CEO's job—risk to self, to fellow employees, to stockholders (owners)?"

I am not much given to the easy-formula approach to executive compensation, and I don't think it would be necessarily in the company's—and by that I mean everyone involved with the company from owner to employee—interest to devise such a system.

The questions for me, then, are, Should we do something about this highly visible issue of executive pay? and, if so, How?

The first question is easy. Of course we should do something about it, although I should be quick to point out that "we" can do very little about it. This is a job for boards of directors, or the owners, of the companies for which the executive works. So my advice is for those particular governing authorities.

As for federal or state government intervention, I am wholeheartedly against it. If easy formulas are not the answer, then governmental regulation is surely not the answer. I can't imagine a worse mess than for the government to try to "control" the pay of highly compensated executives, or anyone else for that matter. This subject is not the place for the righteous indignation of politicians who may see an opportunity for support by picking on the fat cats.

Believe me, there is plenty of opportunity for *appropriate* governmental intervention and regulation of business without taking on the pay of individual workers (yes, the CEO is most usually a "worker," or "employee" like the rest of us, only with more risk, responsibility, and compensation).

Where the intervention and regulation must come

from is those systems of governance now in place in most companies—and let's face it, publicly held corporations are the center of most of this debate—in other words, the boards of directors.

I need not reiterate here that many boards are made up of CEOs, and that there has evolved over the years a sort of self-perpetuating escalation of executive pay as these colleagues, in the name of "competitive compensation," kept raising the ante for one another.

But wait a minute. I am not suggesting a conspiracy to line one another's pockets. Nothing of the sort. It's just that a lot of knee-jerk things are done in the name of "competition" or "marketplace pressures," and the escalation of executive pay has been one of them. It has been an evolving ethic among corporations in America, and at worst, it has been careless acceptance of the conventional management wisdom, not complicity in the gouging of stockholders.

Given the history of how boards of directors are comprised, is it reasonable then to think that boards of directors will, of their own accord and without governmental pressure, make real changes in the way top executives are paid? I think so, and the reason is that stockholders—and especially the big institutional investors—will be taking a more active role in electing and communicating with directors. I believe we are already in an era of increasing accountability by boards to stockholders. Witness General Motors and American Express and IBM (better late than never).

What changes should they make? I am not sure, but I

think the only reasonable way to approach compensation in this day and time is to base it on performance of the company.

Sounds good, but even this requires some definition of *performance*. If that performance is to be measured just by quarter-to-quarter earnings, then executives and their companies will be stuck in the same old short-term actions which have so handicapped the flexibility and the long-term planning of so many American corporations.

Performance must be measured on a multidimensional basis. Each board of directors must determine these measurements, of course, but in my view, performance must transcend the short-term profit stuff to include the longer-term factors that not only guarantee survival, but produce growth and opportunity for all stakeholders. (Incidentally, while *stakeholders* may be a currently hip word, it is nonetheless a very important concept.)

If the top executives meet these standards of performance and the company prospers, then I believe the executives deserve appropriate compensation. Okay, okay, there's that word *appropriate* again. This time, it means whatever the board of directors feels is appropriate.

Even if that means several million dollars a year?

Yes. Why doesn't this bother me? Simple. It should be irrelevant to me unless I am a stockholder of the company. I do not believe there is some magically correct number beyond which executives' pay should not rise. For instance, had I invested ten thousand dollars in Disney stock when Michael Eisner took over, I would be a multimillionaire today, and I assure you, I would not be complaining about Mr. Eisner's compensation, even his last year's big cash-out of stock options. He makes that much money because he meets the standards of performance, and the company prospers.

The real measure of the governance at Disney, of course, will come when and if Mr. Eisner does not meet the standards and the company does not prosper. From what I have heard about him and about Disney, I suspect that his compensation would go *down* appropriately.

Still, it is too easy for the public to look at the earnings statement and conclude that the chief executive officer is overpaid. In fact, I find it strange that the media do not complain about the pay of sports stars and entertainers, who also are often simply "employees" of a company, yet will work themselves into a frenzy about the pay of a corporate CEO.

There are those cases—plenty of them, in fact—in which the CEO *is* overpaid compared to the performance of the company. There have been some shameful examples in the past few years.

On the other hand, remembering that performance should be evaluated on a multidimensional basis, the most obvious measurement—the earnings statement— still *may be not the most appropriate standard* in a given year. If, for instance, during a down period, the CEO commits resources that will pay off with new products and a new plan and a good performance in a few years, then the board may decide to compensate the executive based on what is *expected* to happen.

Which brings me to the final point about performance measurement. It should be done over a period of several years, and I believe that short-term bonuses should be placed in an interest-bearing escrow account, as deferred income, upon which a final performance evaluation will be made after a preset number of years. That, more than anything else, would focus executives to be more long-term.

I am sure that, even accepting all this, you still wonder if there should not be some ceiling on executive pay, some figure beyond which it "just doesn't seem right" to pay an executive—or anyone. I do not believe that is true, and I fear that once we begin to "legislate" or regulate individual incomes in the private sector, there will be no stopping it.

Yes, I am concerned about the vast inequities in America, including the concentration of income and wealth. But I think it is more important to concentrate our government efforts on assuring that everyone has opportunities to succeed and provide for themselves a decent life than on assuring that some people don't get paid too much.

Defensively,
Uncle Jim

QUESTIONS

As kids we were told
at some point in the climb
the question would become
"How much money do you want
and what are you willing to do for it?"
A clichéd question, of course,
and as it turned out after thirty years in business,
one I've never heard asked
of anyone anywhere
except in the movies or on TV.
In our early days,
sometimes we asked it of ourselves
as if we had a choice
other than to keep climbing or quit,
not how much money,
but money or no money.

There is the myth,
on campus or in the church
or the union halls
or the congress or the military
or the civil service,
everywhere except in business,
that we can pull back,
let up, slow down, ease off,
that all we have to do
is just decide to take less money.
It is our desire for money,

they think,
that keeps us at the office or on the road
twelve hours a day
six days out of seven.

Listen.
Most of us do our jobs
because we love to do our jobs
and we know only one way to do our jobs.
Take it or leave it.
Yes, the money has its place
in our hierarchy of needs,
as they say,
sometimes a symbol of praise,
sometimes a measure of worth,
sometimes a way to buy time;
as for the questions,
they are always lying there somewhere,
often just below the surface,
but they are never about money.

The Moment of Truth
About Cost-Cutting

As I write this, we seem safely out of the recent recession, so it strikes me as a good time to look back at the fall of 1992 when: (1) the economy still was in a slump, (2) unemployment was unacceptably high, yet (3) corporate profits generally were rising.

Many people wondered at the time how this could be. I do not claim to have all the answers, but a couple of observations seem to me quite obvious. Yet, no one was discussing them at the time.

To begin, in the fall of 1992, a great many of the corporations showing a rise in profits did so *mostly* as a result of cost-cutting, not as a result of higher revenues. Many companies had done an effective job of increasing their margins by reducing overhead—often through drastic action. They cut inventory costs by becoming more efficient in the management of inventories. In some cases, they delayed capital expenditures. The cost of money decreased, of course, with the lowering of interest rates by the Fed. And—this is the one that gets all the publicity—companies cut jobs by the thousands, changing, some people believe forever, the profiles of their work forces.

And there's the rub, which I believe explains a lot of the rest of the economic bad news of the 1989–91 recession and its aftereffects.

In a 1992 issue of a leading business publication, there

were two stories side by side. One of them quoted an economist explaining that this economy is driven by consumer buying activity. "But consumers are cutting debt, improving their balance sheets instead of buying products." He attributed this to fear, "job insecurity."

It seems simple enough to understand that when people see their friends being laid off, when they experience layoffs at their own companies, they become scared that they might be next. They stop spending and start preparing for their own possible unemployment.

The other story quoted a selection of businesspeople who were lamenting that customers are just not spending money. "Until the people start spending money again, the economy can't start moving," they noted. Some of these businesspeople wondered why home sales were slow with the mortgage rate being its lowest in almost thirty years. "Where are the customers?" one retail executive asked.

I kept wanting to shout the answer: "You and your colleagues have laid them off, you dope!"

I didn't say things like that, though, because until now I thought the answers must be more complicated than that. (Plus, it wouldn't have been a very civil response.)

Now I do feel strongly that this was exactly the case. Companies, while patting themselves on the back for their cost-cutting prowess, were a major part of the disillusion and pessimism among consumers. They were, in effect, blithely laying off one another's customers—destroying, obviously, the purchasing power of those people, and scaring the hell out of those who had managed to keep their jobs.

The pattern was dramatic. It seems that, as soon as the consumer confidence index began to blip upward, some big company announced major layoffs, and people hunkered down again and the index dropped.

Of course, the economic situation was and is complicated, but I don't know anyone who disagrees that the key to a good economy is consumer confidence, which turns people into customers.

Now back to those corporate profits. The question then and now is, Now what? How deep can a company cut costs and not sacrifice its growth? (I suspect some already have sacrificed growth for the short-term profit improvement.)

One of my mentors in business used to say, "You can't cost-cut your way to success, except in the very short term, and even then you need to be damned careful."

What this means is that, at some point, profits *must* be driven by revenues. If the economy does not pick up dramatically for these companies, will they continue to try to cut costs, will they lay off even more of one another's customers? Who knows what would happen then?

Who knows how long the current good news about the economy will last? Who knows what really to expect from the current administration's economic policies? I can only hope that the economy will stay truly strong and the layoffs will stop. At that point, with renewed consumer demand, we'll find out which companies achieved the right balance between overhead and revenues. In other words, which companies were sensible enough to bear the costs of being ready to respond, versus those which cost-cut themselves out of business.

At that moment of truth, we might well be asking how it could be that (1) the economy is on a rise, (2) unemployment is declining to a more bearable level, yet (3) some corporate profits are down. We'll see.

Finding the Spirit in Business

There has been in the past several years a great upsurge in the numbers of people who describe themselves as "religious" or "spiritual." The religious institutions concern themselves, quite naturally, with how this wave of spirituality will play itself out in the churches or if it will make a difference at all in church membership and attendance and participation.

My curiosity has more to do with how people's perception of their spirituality and its impact on their behavior will be felt in the community of business and work.

It is not an overstatement to say that a wave of spiritual expression is beginning to sweep over business, reflecting even in the vocabulary. When *Love and Profit,* my book about "caring leadership" was published in 1991, the words *love* and *caring* used in a business context were considered curiosities if not downright weird. In at least half of my media appearances, I had to smile through bad jokes connecting the title of the book with the world's oldest profession. Or I was met with total skepticism about the efficacy of managers treating their employees with love and caring.

How times change, and how quickly.

Now we hear such words as *covenant, community, servant leadership,* and, with a more secular turn, *personal growth* used in everyday business language. Some managers begin their meetings with a few minutes of meditative silence. One manager of my acquaintance in a Fortune 100 company makes personal growth one of the performance standards in his group.

Frankly, I welcome the wave, and I hope it sweeps further and faster throughout the business community. On the other hand, the concepts of religion and spirituality in business have, as do many other concepts, their dangers.

Partly as a result of *Love and Profit,* I have been asked to give speeches and conduct workshops for religious groups and business groups with some religious connection. (My Baptist-preacher father may be turning over in his grave.)

But I am honest with these groups, right from the beginning. I tell them that, frankly, I do not claim expertise in the realm of spirituality, except perhaps my own; I claim no particular insights about theology or religion; I claim only to know a great deal about management, the workplace, people within that workplace, how they treat one another, and how they should treat one another.

Then, without intending to shock my audience, I'm afraid I often do just that when I say I shudder a little every time I hear a businessperson say, "We run our business according to Christian principles."

I shudder because I think those so-called Christian principles are more often used for restricting or policing than for liberating and enabling.

Most of those business people, in my observation, usually are talking about prescribed standards of behavior which, as we know, are often confused with Christian principles.

I always want to ask, "By operating according to Christian principles, do you mean that you make extraordinary efforts to love your neighbor, to love your enemy (competition), to feed the poor, to heal the sick, to turn the other cheek when you've been wronged? Are you more concerned with the 'least of these,' or the 'richest of these'?"

Frankly, I don't want to offend these folks, but I do prefer that business, particularly in these days of increasing diversity, not try to project any one sectarian view *institutionally*. This does not mean, of course, that I do not admire those business people who try to conduct their lives in accordance with their personal beliefs.

So just where do I think business should place itself in the debate about spirituality and belief in the workplace?

Fundamentally, I believe that business must be held to ethical standards and must live out and project those ethical standards among all its stakeholders: owners, employees, customers, vendors, and the community at large.

Ethical standards, I hasten to point out, are always born of the moral standards of the people in business, and those moral standards often derive from religious belief. I like to say that there are no business ethics, only people ethics, because business does not exist in some abstract way but is revealed and enacted through people and only through people.

So there are two challenges for business in the realm of ethics and ethical behavior:

First is the challenge to do good and do well at the same time.

The second is to recognize, understand, and encourage

the concept that employees must have a working environment in which they can grow personally and, yes, spiritually. I believe that much spiritual growth is possible through the doing of business because of the simple fact that the doing of business requires interaction with our fellow human beings, and within those interactions are vast possibilities for spiritual connection and growth.

In addition, I believe that work can become a spiritual discipline when people do what they have set themselves to do with an abiding sense of excellence, not only in the results they achieve, but also in the very effort itself.

These notions are difficult to make concrete within the business environment because, despite the professed religiosness of so many people, there is considerably more trust in, and reliance on, the external world than on the internal world.

It is the rare leader—business or government—who is willing to redefine reality. In fact, the most frequent response to something based in any unconventional approach to a business situation is to say, "Well, that sounds like a nice idea, but the reality is . . ." Reality is always defined externally, and most often by the flow of money rather than of ideas.

Let me use a concrete example. When I discuss employing disabled people, the response has often been, "Well, that's a noble idea and I'm all for it but, the reality is . . ."

It has taken the Americans with Disabilities Act (ADA) to change these "realities." And even now, businesspeople are saying, "Well, the ADA is a nice idea, but the reality is that the trial lawyers are going to make a mint off all the lawsuits."

In my view, of course, the reality is that the ADA, though forced on business, is the perfect example of how to do good and do well, how to positively impact the work environment, and how to expand the concept of the community of work. Some, including me, might say that it is also an institutional expression of religious principles.

Rather than bragging about how "we run our business according to such-and-such principles," I'd prefer to paraphrase Vaclav Havel's famous quote and say: The salvation of business (he said *the world*) lies in the human heart.

At this point, you might be asking, "If you're so damned smart, how would you make the changes you believe should happen?"

I have no perfect answer, but just as I believe business must be done by, for, and among people, I believe both challenges—to do good and to do well, and to allow a place for personal and spiritual growth—must result from the environment that is created

That's why, in my consulting and speaking with managers and leaders, I start with the belief that the first requirement of the leader is self-awareness. This comes through the inner life and through nothing external, except to the extent that external things stimulate or inform or inspire the inner life.

What the self-awareness must lead to is a letting go: a letting go of the illusion of control and a letting go of ego, both of which mean a letting go of—or a change in—the concept of—power.

This results in a way of treating people that emphasizes, above anything else, honesty, trust, and special treatment according to people's individual special human needs. To do that requires a manager or leader of great courage, because this inevitably means that the leader must see himself or herself not as a boss but as a resource, or in the words of the late business consultant and professor Robert K. Greenleaf, a "servant."

Some people have told me that what I say on this subject sounds very Christian. It is my impression that the basic human-to-human teachings of most religions do not differ radically from one another, but it may be that, because I have been raised in the Christian tradition, the things I say naturally sound Christian.

But let me assure you of one thing: You'll never hear me brag about how I run my business according to Christian principles. I'll just let people judge that for themselves.

The "Big Bloom Theory"

Dear Art:

I have a poet friend who, in the interest of making our language less violent, urges scientists to stop referring to the "Big Bang Theory" (which my friend with poetic license calls the "Big Boom Theory"), suggesting instead that they call it the "Big Bloom Theory."

His notion, which makes sense to me, is that God is very likely more involved with the blossoming of life in its infinite variety throughout the universe than with the blowing apart of matter.

The point, of course, has less to do with the beginning, being, and becoming of the universe than with the ways we, particularly in this most "advanced" nation of ours, choose to refer to any number of happenings, both momentous as well as mundane.

It certainly is not news that sports and business often become the psychological equivalents of war. You've heard me on that subject for years. I believe that now in 1994, the news is the extent to which the vocabulary of anger, violence, and hate permeates our national discussions, beyond sports and business to politics and public policy, the arts, education, even the church.

Some personal examples:

"We have to train our guns on the problem." Said by a university president at a board meeting.

"We kicked a little butt tonight." Said by a president of the United States about a political campaign.

"We're going to waste those bastards." Attributed to

an athlete commenting about a coming game. (*Game?*) Other phrases also gleaned from the sports pages: "Kill them." "Blow them away." "Annihilate them."

And I do not need to reiterate here some of the hate lyrics of popular music.

"So you're one of the baby-killers." Said by one delegate to a fellow delegate at the 1992 Iowa Republican Convention. I could go on and on about the violence of campaign rhetoric in 1992. Never, it seems to me, was it so mean-spirited.

Lately, I've wondered if we are losing our ability as a society to respect other viewpoints, to simply be *civil* to one another.

When people supposedly representing churches or a religious viewpoint practice violence, in language and deed, in order to put forth their beliefs, then we have come to a bad state, indeed.

When business people lose sight of the concepts of fair competition and speak of "destroying the competition," of "putting them out of business," of "leaving them bloodied and battered," of "taking no prisoners," of "putting them in an awful lot of hurt"—all quotes I've heard or read in the business press—then those business people have lost sight of the deeper purposes of business.

Where did all this nastiness come from anyway? Some say the Saturday morning cartoons. Others say television or the movies. "The Pop Culture" generally gets its share of blame along with rock and roll and rap.

I don't know, but I suspect there is plenty of blame to go around. Clearly, I am not impressed by those politicians and other leaders who rail against the popular culture then talk about "killing" their opponents in the election.

I don't know to what extent our preoccupation with the vocabulary of violence is a cause or effect in our society and world, but I am a strong believer in the proposition that we *are* what we *say,* and that the first step toward changing the way we *are* is to change the way we *talk* about it.

To do that, we have always depended on our institutional leaders, in politics, in business, in the media, to set the standards of language and civility, to be in effect our national role models. These role models have now fallen in short supply, so perhaps we are left only to our own devices, to face this problem as individuals. Which, come to think of it, may be the best way.

We can, one person at a time, try to change vocabularies and influence other people, one at a time.

With that thought, Art, why don't you and I join my poet friend in talking about the "Big Bloom Theory." It's a start.

Love,
Dad

OF CORPORATIONS
AND COMMUNION

Adapted for my friends at Murdoch Magazines,
Sydney, Australia

In a way,
the good people are still with us,
all those you can name
plus many you never knew.
They are part of this celebration
which as we know
is not about careers and accomplishments
but about life itself,
life and the two things that keep us living,
relationships and work,
the people we love and the things we love to do.
So, many of those who have gone before
are here,
and in a way,
so are the ones who are still to come,
even those not yet born.
"How can that be?" you ask.
Consider this:
Life and work and love in any setting,
even a corporation,
can be acts of communion
transcending all of us who pass through,
with our only hope being
that when we retire or take our leave,
we have left something of ourselves,

enough that part of us will be there always.
"And how do we do that?" you ask.
Listen.
Work, those things we have set ourselves to do,
is like everything else in life,
and our chance for immortality
comes only through what we have done
to help other people.
Some of us succeed, some of us don't.

If in a business enterprise we could,
as in the church,
attach special spiritual significance
to those who succeed,
if we could build shrines or dedicate holy places,
if we could but call them
teacher or master, prophet or saint,
there might be words available,
a vocabulary of praise we could use
to commemorate what they have done.
But we are reduced to this:
They will always be here.

And so, we pray,
may we all.

GETTING THROUGH THE STACK

There was a sales manager in Chicago
who would sit at his dining table
and color maps,
a different color for each territory,
then he would take them to the office,
where they would become the marching orders
for his platoon of salespeople.
One time when the children in school
were telling what their fathers did,
his daughter said, "He colors maps."
He quit after that,
saying that the measure of any job
should be how a child describes it,
moved west and bought a little newspaper,
something he could hold in his hands every week.

It's easy for me to understand why he quit,
as I sit at my desk early
before anyone else is in,
moving the paperwork
carefully, thoughtfully, deliberately
from my IN box
across the desk where I sign
or initial or write notes in the margins,
to my OUT box,
one stack getting smaller, the other larger,

and I can measure the change,
that simple act satisfying me
more than anything I will do all day.
It is the most tangible
yet the least of what I am to do.

BIG NEWS

The game is won by those
who learn the news before everyone else.
The game has no name
but it is pursued seriously
and is taken as a measure
of a person's involvement in "the industry."
(It reminds me of nothing so much
as small-town gossip
with each industry a different small town.)
One day in New York
our industry was abuzz.
One of our competitor companies was shutting down,
selling its properties one by one.
All morning in our halls nothing but speculation
about people and products
and where they would go.
All but lost was the news
that one of our secretaries,
unmarried and no doubt scared,
had decided to have the baby
and had chosen this day
to let us in on it.
It would have been big news for our group
on any other day,
but today the game was on
and news like that gets no points.

ON TRYING TO WRITE A NOTE
TO AN EMPLOYEE WHOSE
BABY DIED OF SIDS

I have written a million little notes,
by hand on these personal pads,
about new jobs and promotions and raises,
about babies born,
about triumphs of all kinds
from college degrees to bowling trophies.
And I have written, of course,
about deaths in the family.
But there are times
when I know that anything I say will fall short,
when any word I choose will be wrong.

I think now of my little boy
so few years ago in his crib
and how I would check him in the night,
fearful as ever that good things
live always in peril,
cupping my hand around his head,
watching for the breaths
which it seemed to me
could so easily stop,
and I think of how it would have felt

to wait for a breath
that did not come again.

Words will never do,
and even my tears on this blank sheet
will have no meaning for her.

FREEDOM

They were putting a glass skin on the building,
a giant one-way mirror
behind which we in our offices
could watch the world
but nobody out there could watch us.
It was to save energy, they said,
so bear with the noise
and the distraction of men hanging outside our windows.
We got so used to it
we would tuck in our shirttails
or rearrange our underwear
or do those other private little things
people do when they think no one is watching.
One day, a different movement, a fluttering
pulled me to the window.
There, on the sill, a pigeon.
It tried to fly through the one-way mirror
but was driven upward by the glass,
then sideways
from one office windowsill to another.
It would disappear from my view and return,
then finally, along with it, came people
following the pigeon from office to office,
some shooing it with their hands
and encouraging it with words,
"Fly down. Down. Dive. It's closed at the top,"
as if they could explain the logic
of the construction to the pigeon.

One man, a literary sort,
began to talk about it as a metaphor.
"The sun and sky and freedom are an illusion.
He can't get to them the obvious way."
The man was right, of course,
but knowing how not to get there
was not enough for the pigeon
who with each try became weaker
until it fluttered to the sill below
and the one below
and out of sight.

I like to think
that when it fell at last
below where the men were working
and realized it had stumbled onto freedom,
it still had the strength
to make another start.

RETIREMENT

It is early.
Six-thirty.
The building is quiet.
I came in to write letters
and to pack.
Soon the place will come to life,
as it always does,
with the rush of people working.

These days, though, it's the smaller, slower things
I notice:
the droning of fans and compressors,
keeping us warm or cool,
the buzz of fluorescent lights,
the burble of the big percolator
and the smell of coffee,
the talk of the secretaries outside my door,
or a sudden laugh halfway down the hall.

As the time here grows shorter,
I find myself thinking of other times
when I could not wait for the day, or the week,
to be over,
the times I strained toward Christmas or a vacation,
an exquisite few days away from it all.
I think of meetings that would never end,
of hours stuck on a taxiway,
airliners lined up as far as I could see,

of those eternal minutes right before someone
was to come into my office
to be fired.

I understand now why every writer who ever lived
wrote about time and its paradoxes.
And everything they ever said
about how fast time passes is true.
But they never told us how many slow days
we would have to endure
before we realized how fast they had gone.

Part Two

Men and Women at Work

Women Can Change
the "How" of What We Do

Dear Art:

You asked, "Where is all that 'nurturing' women were supposed to bring to the workplace?"

But maybe the question should be, "How hospitable has business been to the nurturing they wanted to bring?"

We know that some of the women who are veterans of business tried to—and perhaps had to—follow the male role models. Some say it is because there were no women role models, and these same observers point out that there still are not all that many women role models in the very top positions (the "glass ceiling" commentary).

Nonetheless, I'm optimistic about women moving to the top, and because I'm optimistic about that, I'm also optimistic about business. You see, business needs what women bring to the running of companies.

But be careful how you define *nurturing,* and please don't let all that talk of nurture fool you into thinking that women are pushovers, that they are not brave enough to do the difficult things of management. More than changing *what* must be done, they will change *how* it is done.

I have already seen how women, in their inclination to affiliate, to bond, bring a different tone to almost any transaction. Even those women described as "tough," who seem to work hard at the old "tough guy" model of management, still bring to their toughness a willingness to connect rather than hiding behind the mask of toughness as men so frequently do.

I've had the opportunity lately to associate with women in many different companies, and when I lecture and give workshops on caring leadership, the women get it quickly, well before the men. I believe the different responses represent simply the willingness of women to reach out, to reveal their feelings, to connect, to bond— all of which we've heard so much about—and the men's fear of those things. Understand that there are exceptions and that I am consciously generalizing. Understand also that, even in my generalizations, I do not condemn the men as not capable of connecting, but it seems to require a much greater effort for them to let go and do it.

These differences are manifest, I believe, in many ways—large and small—on the job.

You've heard me talk about the woman manager who translated her skills as a parent into being a manager? Let me give you another, quite different, example which makes the point about what women bring.

I like to take your nine-year-old brother Ronald to the airport to watch airplanes. We now have a radio for monitoring the conversation between the traffic controllers and the pilots.

A few weeks ago, a woman was doing the tower traffic controller duty. That's the person in charge of the movement of all airplanes within the airspace of the airport. The tower operator clears the planes for takeoff and for landing, and monitors their progress in the traffic pattern. It's a high-pressure job.

On this particular day, there was the usual hectic scene. The Air National Guard was flying their A-7 fighters; the airliners were coming and going; the private pilots were out in force in their light planes. The place was like a beehive, which for Ronald, of course, was the best of all situations.

Speaking as a former jet fighter pilot, I can testify that the woman tower operator did a magnificent job. Yet, it was different in a very significant way.

For example, there was a private pilot in a Cessna. He was to land, but did not have the field in sight. A man in the tower would most probably have adopted a stern voice, and the Cessna pilot would have been intimidated into *not* admitting that he did not see the field. This would have put the pilot's macho image at risk, you see.

But the woman controller said, simply and gently, "Cessna seven seven six Bravo Charley (I changed the number), if you don't see the airport, call when you get closer and I'll help you."

He did. She did. He landed safely and that was that.

When a plane took off, she'd say, "United five seventy-six, contact departure control. See ya, and have a great flight."

And to a flight of national guard fighters in close formation approaching to land: "Lookin' pretty good up there."

And to the pilot of a Mooney who normally flies for American Airlines and had his nephew in the plane: "Bring him to the tower after you land. We'll show him around."

The whole tone and spirit of the exchanges were different. Everyone seemed to enjoy it. Yet, the job was done effectively and efficiently.

Do I credit this goodwill, this effectiveness, this reassuring tone to the mere fact that the tower operator was a woman?

You bet I do. And there's a big lesson there for business.

Your sister, Clare, will be part of changing business and part of that redirection of energy not only from *what* we do but also to *how* we do it. I hope you and a lot of other men are paying attention.

Love,
Dad

Redefining the "Other"

Dear Clare:

You asked how I became a feminist. It's not as easy a question to answer as I thought. The quick answer is that I am a civil libertarian, and though true, this strikes me as a little too glib. I could also say, as a businessman, that feminism is important to business, but that explanation would also be incomplete.

In answering, I must reflect on my upbringing as a Southerner, my years as a jet fighter pilot, my troubled marriages, and my episodes of being a predatory romantic.

So shall we call this letter the "confessions of a racist, sexist homophobe?" That would not be entirely accurate, but sometimes when I think about the things I've said or done or of the opinions I've held, I shudder. "If I'm so damned smart," I ask myself, "how could I have been so stupid?"

Easy. It's easy to do and believe stupid things in this world because our most basic inclination is to like people who are like us and to fear people who are not like us. Including, in my case, women.

What I have come to understand is the dramatic connection between racism and sexism and homosexism (I know this is not the proper word, but it strikes me as more apt than *homophobia*).

Hitler understood it, too. His pronouncements and Nazi literature were filled with condemnation of other races, of homosexuals, and by implication, of women.

One of the undesirable characteristics of Jews, according to Hitler, was that they were "effeminate," a word which long ago lost its neutrality and became a term of derision.

On the other hand, the great spiritual leaders, in their understanding of the fears and misunderstandings about "the other," recognized that we often *define ourselves* only in context with other people. We are what they are not.

I believe this is why Jesus, when asked to explain whom he meant when he said love thy neighbor, told the story of The Good Samaritan. It was the consummate story of "the other." These days the story could be entitled, "The Good Gang Member" or "The Good Fundamentalist" or "The Good Liberal," depending, of course, on the audience.

I confess that, as a child in the South, I accepted all the conventional wisdom about the lesser intelligence, the lower standards of hygiene, the looser sexual mores, the laziness, and the generally antisocial behavior of African Americans (then called "nigras" by the "nice" people and worse names by everyone else).

I confess also that, as a teenager, I felt it was my duty to try to have sex with every girl who seemed in the slightest inclined to do so. Of course, I wanted to marry the ones who remained "nice." Young boys of my generation actually devoted great portions of their conversation to discussing the merits of marrying a virgin, and how to tell when you had succeeded at it. I was listening to older boys talk about a girl's first sexual experience before I had any notion of what a hymen was.

As for homosexuals, I listened to the older boys talk about beating up and robbing homosexuals simply because they were homosexuals. (I wrote your brother Art another letter about this.) Though I never did such a thing, it seemed okay to me because the homosexuals were "asking for it" by virtue of their sexual orientation just as some girls were "asking" to be "felt up" or harassed by what clothes they wore or how they looked at a boy or how close they danced or some other perceived sexual behavior.

Why do I go into all this? Maybe it's my Baptist background and I want to testify to the fact of redemption, or maybe it's just that I want to make sure you or no one else thinks that I came to my present beliefs from a sheltered environment. The past twenty-five years have been a difficult journey, one that has led me, without equivocation, to become dedicated to the cause of civil and human rights.

One very conservative business colleague suggested to me, in the midst of a lively discussion, that he heard penance in my voice, that he heard the result of my own feelings of guilt. He was proud of his point only long enough for me to say, "Damned right, you hear guilt! I *am* guilty, and it is time for a lot of us to admit it."

But I am *not* trying to do penance; I am just trying to do the right thing. And I include doing the right thing for business.

What it gets down to are questions of talent and opportunity. Do we want to use all the talent available to us as we try to compete in the new global economy? If so, how are we going to assure that everyone has equal social, economic, and professional opportunities to use their talents in the pursuit of happiness for themselves, and productive work for their business enterprises and for society?

You'd think the answer to the first question would be self-evident: a resounding "yes!" But think about it. The question focuses on *talent,* not on gender or race or ethnic background or sexual orientation or anything else which has, throughout our history, identified people as "the other."

Unfortunately, there is little evidence to suggest that business traditionally has opened itself to talent without regard for "the other." In fact, there was stubborn resistance to "the other" until the civil rights movement, then the feminist movement, the gay rights movement, and more recently, the people with disabilities movement.

So we in business have had trouble even getting to question number two. We've been too busy defining the kind of people we don't want to work with—their perceived morals, their perceived competence, their perceived work habits, their perceived emotional stability— to stop and examine what talents they bring to our enterprises.

A CEO of a major corporation told me once, "I know it doesn't sound good but, for whatever reason, I just don't like to be around homosexuals."

I didn't bother to ask him how he knew who was homosexual and who was not. He was talking about male homosexuals, of course, and he meant he was uncomfortable around men who are effeminate (remember that word?).

I noticed also that not one key person on his staff was

female or African American. I don't think it was mere coincidence.

Things change, of course, and business is changing rapidly, partly because of the laws and partly because more and more business people are seeing the efficacy of focusing on talent and ability and not on other defining factors.

You see, Clare, the whole idea that there can somehow be social justice without economic justice is sheer nonsense. We cannot give "the others" their rights as citizens then restrict their rights to make money along with the rest of "us." And we cannot require that "the others" give up their identities and try to become like "us" in order to gain access to the opportunities.

In one of my first management positions, I remember making decisions about hiring salaries by considering whether the new person was male or female, single or married. We always started a married man at a higher salary than a single woman—*even when the woman's job required more education or experience.* What a thing for a feminist to have to admit! And the inequity of it never even crossed my mind (needless to say, I was a married man with two young children).

Those pay inequities did not exist between white employees and African American employees—we did not have any black employees until years later.

As for the homosexuals, there was an unacknowledged agreement: They'd keep their sexual orientation in the closet and we would pretend we didn't know.

Business has come a long way since those days, further,

in fact, than most other sectors of society, but still not far enough.

So I continue to talk about the role of management in creating a workplace that is a community of work in which people can grow personally and spiritually as well as professionally and financially. And I continue to share my own experiences and what I have learned about how we sacrifice our own potential by limiting the potential of anyone else.

You remember the Pogo slogan, "We have spotted the enemy and they are us"? (Of course not, you're too young.) Well, try this one: We have spotted the others and they are us.

With love from your idealistic, starry-eyed, bleeding-heart, knee-jerk do-gooder (oh, yes, one of *those* others) . . .

Dad

Another Theory
About Sexual Harassment

In the paper this morning, there was yet another story about a man in a position of authority who abused his power and betrayed a trust by having a sexual relationship with a woman who respected and trusted him (and perhaps was infatuated with him) *because* of his position.

We see it all the time, it seems: priests and ministers; therapists, counselors, and physicians; and of course, politicians, business executives, and managers. Reputations ruined, careers devastated, lives disrupted, and in some cases, destroyed.

Though I have displayed plenty of sexist attitudes over the years, I read the news and cluck my tongue.

Why does it happen? Why would people indulge in such bizarre and aberrant behavior? Even if ethics and morality weren't issues, why in the world would these professional people take such risks? As an ancillary question, why would sexual harassment continue to be such a problem in the workplace after all the attention it has received?

I don't know, but I have a theory. I confess up front that my theory comes purely from a male observer's viewpoint. And I must say that while I have heard about women using their power and position to harass and exploit men, I just have not personally witnessed it.

It strikes me that the problem is at least 95 percent one of men as predator and women as prey.

Which, if you believe my theory, makes sense. I'm sure this theory will not stand the heat of scientific scrutiny, but here goes.

With few exceptions in the animal kingdom, especially among primates, the strongest males, the "dominant males" are those who by virtue of their position of power are rewarded by mating with the females. In other words, they are powerful, so they get the sex.

The popular culture, of course, offers convincing if anecdotal evidence in support of this theory. Consider the highly publicized sexual exploits of celebrities, from rock stars to actors to athletes, with perhaps the most extravagant example being Wilt Chamberlain's claim to having had sex with several thousand women during his career (so far).

Strangely enough, the public seems to accept rather benignly this behavior, almost the way the old primate group or tribe accepted the sexual privileges of the dominant males.

But the standard apparently changes when applied to those perceived to be somehow in the public trust—including businesspeople (excluding perhaps Donald Trump, who seems to have crossed over from business to pop culture). The public is far less tolerant of the behavior of politicians like Gary Hart and Robert Packwood, and there is no tolerance at all for professionals—doctors, lawyers, therapists, clergy—who violate the trust of those in their care.

And in expounding on this theory, I am not suggesting acceptance or tolerance of destructive behaviors. It is just that I do think we men are conditioned to believe that our positions of power, authority, or status qualify us for special rewards. These rewards, whether they are money, property, fame, respect, or simple admiration, can lead us to believe that we deserve even greater rewards. It sort of feeds on itself.

Added to that is an incredible ability to rationalize our way into anything, based on all the obvious rewards we have received, rewards which in themselves are public evidence that we are damned good and deserving. We get to believing we can do no wrong or that, if we do, it will always be for the right reasons, which of course makes it seem less than wrong.

Now comes a woman who is drawn in one way or another to our success and position. We are flattered by her attention, and she, because of her own personal issues, may be vulnerable to and flattered by our attention.

In my observation, men who err in this situation respond in one of two general ways. The most pernicious are the men who somehow need to harass and exploit women as a constant expression of power. They are *always* "hitting on" women. These are the men who are at the extreme of my theory; they don't really feel they have power at all unless they can demonstrate it to themselves through sexual conquest.

The second group are those men who, while they may be able all their lives to overcome evolutionary tradition or custom or—who knows?—even genetic programming by applying their intellect and values to effect respect and integrity in their behavior toward women, simply slip.

The reasons they revert to what I think of as the "animal self" are too complicated for me to grasp and are best left to the psychologists and psychiatrists.

But it is no big surprise to me that sex finds its way into the status and power picture. Considering our natural history, we might well express satisfaction that so few men of power, influence, and authority give in to these instincts and sexually exploit women. Given our animal selves, we might well wonder what is the point of fame, power, influence, and wealth if there is no sexual payoff?

Fortunately, however, we have *for the most part* evolved into rational, intellectual, and spiritual creatures who can redefine for themselves what the conditions and rewards of a successful life should be without exploiting anyone else.

The Subject Is Still Sex

Sure, there have been a lot of changes in the workplace; sure, women are more evident, are more forceful, are more present at higher levels. Yet, we have not made the progress we should.

I'm not talking about the obvious areas like not enough women CEOs, not enough women in senior management positions, not enough women on boards of directors, or not enough women in governance generally, and so on. I'm talking about the day-to-day workplace stuff, the ubiquitous man-woman interactions. We still have a long way to go.

Why? I'm not sure, but I think it probably is the same old problem: sex.

No, I don't mean the overt, destructive behaviors such as sexual exploitation or sexual harassment, neither of which is about sex, but about power.

I'm talking about something more benign, but still risky. Sex itself. Of course, I believe managers must be alert to problems of sexual harassment and other forms of inappropriate or negative sexual behavior in the workplace. Nonetheless, we would be foolish not to recognize and admit that the workplace offers a fertile medium for sexual tension, including positive sexual attraction on both sides of the gender gap—then try to figure out ways to address it.

We begin with the incontrovertible truth that it is incredibly difficult for men and women to maintain friendships that achieve any degree of intimacy and trust without there also being either sexual overtones or, simply, a sexual relationship. Once that happens, of course, particularly if it happens outside the accepted societal norms—an extramarital relationship, for example—the "friendship" has changed in tone and content forever. Furthermore, the intimacy that the friends had intended most often becomes another kind of intimacy altogether.

I speak from experience. It took me at least forty years to be able to establish a true friendship with a woman, one of trust, intimacy, love, and support, *without* using sex as a crutch.

Until recently, I believed that the generation behind me, the young, informed, thoughtful generation of babyboomers would not have that difficulty. Not true. And the "sexual revolution" apparently did not help.

Professional and work interactions seem just as difficult for them as they were for me. Although in a company, these relationships have a structure in which to operate and rules and policies to guide them—at least on the surface—sexual tension nevertheless informs them. I have watched this process, and participated in it, for thirty-two years. I've kept expecting it to change; it has not.

What to do? Frankly, there is just so much that can be done. On the one hand, it is good for fellow employees to care about one another and to support one another. Given that reality, it is also true that the pressures of a man and woman working together on a particularly intense project, and the joy that comes with completing that project successfully, produces feelings much akin to those in a romantic love relationship. How natural then that, in this environment, sexual attraction can enter the picture.

If there are no marriages involved, the situation may take whatever course the participants feel is appropriate in accordance with their own values, given good judgment about behavior at the workplace and impact on fellow workers.

If, as is too often the case, there are marriage partners at home, the trouble begins.

Please understand that I don't feel it is the manager's role to be the arbiter of morality, and I don't think it is the manager's role to probe—only to respond if asked for advice.

So here are the big questions:

1. How can the company create an atmosphere in which these situations are most readily avoided?

2. To what extent can the individual manager create an atmosphere in which these situations are avoided?

3. What can the people themselves do to create an atmosphere in which these situations are avoided?

Answer to question number 1: Unless companies become committed to a whole new ethic about this problem, the answer is, "They probably can't." While there may not be any institutional way to completely prevent sexual relationships ("affairs") among employees, there *are* ways to change the vocabulary of these discussions and to provide a forum for them. It is a matter, I believe, of saying that "we recognize the inherent possibilities for personal involvements as a result of intense mutual involvement in your work, so we want to provide counseling and assistance to anyone who feels he or she needs it."

That counseling and assistance can be through an Employees' Assistance Program (EAP) of individual counseling and therapy, or through facilitating open discussion between the people who feel themselves at risk, or who are actually in this situation.

At present, too many companies, lacking a more thoughtful and helpful policy, fire the participants as soon as they find out about an "affair," depending, I suppose, on fear to serve as a deterrent to others. Of course, that ignores the fact that if the lovers ever thought anyone, including the company, was likely to find out, they might have been more discreet, but they almost certainly would *not* have avoided the relationship. We Americans hold to the particularly compelling romantic myth that these things "just happen."

Most other companies try to "look the other way" and let the participants work it out themselves. Or the EAP takes over with counseling and assistance.

Without creating the atmosphere, vocabulary, and forum for prevention, however, all the rest of it is after the fact and, at best, is little more than damage control.

Answer to question number 2: Unless managers commit themselves to creating an environment of open discussion and a "safe place" for employees to explore and find solutions to an impending problem, the answer is, "a little, but still not much." Too many managers, I'm afraid, play the private-eye game from time to time, trying to catch people doing something wrong, but that is largely ineffective. Other managers try to play the Dutch-uncle role, intervening with "words to the wise," strictly off the record of course. I don't criticize these managers for trying, but again, it's all after the fact.

Creating an atmosphere of open discussion is quite difficult for managers, of course, simply because any discussion of sex or sexual tension in the workplace, beyond good and important education about sexual harassment, is both personally and legally risky. But it can be done if boundaries are clearly understood up front, if a professional counselor is made part of the process, and if all parties agree to a discussion.

Answer to question number 3: "A lot." I don't just mean taking the personal responsibility for one's own behavior, as we all should, but also creating a relationship of openness, honesty, respect, and integrity toward fellow workers. The answer, I believe, lies in an atmosphere in which both men and women recognize that in the community of work, in the intensity and dedication with which they engage their work, they have a truly special relationship. The more effective they are in their work together, the more special the relationship becomes. The more special the relationship becomes, the more likely it can take on personal dimensions which bond people together in ways that have within them the inherent risk of romantic and sexual attachments.

This is best avoided by open and honest discussion of the possibilities and of personal vulnerabilities.

That too is risky, but it is far better than doing what we've always done and pretending the problem does not exist or that it won't happen in our group.

It's time to stop thinking that as men and women become accustomed to working together, "professional standards and behavior" will prevail, and the risk of sexual involvement will then go away. Rather, we should understand, admit, and shine the light of instructive discussion on the reality that professionalism and sexual attraction are far from mutually exclusive.

We cannot let the fear of sexual harassment charges keep this subject off the agenda and under the rug where it has been for too long.

THE SEXUAL REVOLUTION

My little part of the sexual revolution
had its start in a dark and crowded bar
where all the up-and-coming businessmen
met the women who came to meet
the up-and-coming businessmen.
La Boucherie it was called,
with butcher block tables and steaks
(the meat market pun lost on no one),
a kind of Shangri La for men
who did not want to go home
to all those obligations
that robbed them of their manhood,
who felt free among the people
of *La Boucherie*,
the turtlenecked, blazered, and blow-dried real estate guys,
the miniskirted Delta stewardesses,
tan from their San Juan layovers
(always emphasizing the *lay* in layovers)
We were Strangers in the Night,
transformed by Witchcraft,
and carried Up Up and Away
in one another's Beautiful Balloons,
coming down much later
in our swamp of lies and anger,
our resolutions and promises lasting
only until the next evening at five.

One Man's Opinion About Work and Homosexual Rights

Dear Art:

I'm proud of you. It took courage to speak out for the rights of homosexuals to serve in the military. I understand your disappointment at having your opinion called irrelevant because you've never served in the military.

And yes, some of your adversaries in that discussion probably *do* now think you are a "closet gay." I know it's difficult to tell yourself, *So what?*—but sometimes there is no other way to respond to those who cannot accept a differing view without looking for the hidden agendas. We live increasingly in an age of fear and distrust, an age in which rational differences of opinion are just not accepted, in which reality is defined by prejudice and not objective consideration.

This is not to say that everyone who opposes military service for homosexuals is a narrow-minded bigot. To the contrary, reasonable people may disagree on this as on many subjects.

Regardless of last summer's compromise between President Clinton and the Pentagon, this issue appears now to be on a long, tortuous and, I fear, sometimes violent road toward resolution, no matter what you and I think, but since you asked my opinion specifically about homosexuals and the military, I'll respond. Then I have a few other thoughts to add.

To begin, my attitude on this subject cannot be limited to the military. I include the business world, as well. When it comes to matters of discrimination in employment practices, the same rules should apply to everyone. While businesspeople may not personally be enthusiastic about employment rights for homosexuals, the legal issues are, for the most part, determined.

Thus, I believe we should not exclude the military by making it a "special case" based on largely emotional arguments.

One of those arguments is that if homosexuals are allowed in the military, people (they used to say *men*) just won't be able to "bond" the way they must in order to be effective in combat.

My first response: *Who* says? How do they know? Has anyone observed this lack of "bonding"? Has anyone conferred about this with military leaders of other countries who do allow homosexuals to serve?

Second response: The great majority of people in the military will *never* see combat. And never have. Not close enough to require the legendary "bonding" anyway. In fact, most military jobs are noncombat jobs. So what's the problem? Does this mean we have to be afraid that homosexuals will prevent the steno pool or supply clerks or data-entry specialists or motor-pool drivers from "bonding," thus threatening our national security?

Another argument is that if homosexuals are allowed in our all-volunteer military, the straight people won't volunteer, and we'll lose effectiveness.

My first response: So we should make our military a

haven for those who don't want to work with homosexuals?

Second response: Those folks who might otherwise volunteer but don't for this reason will have a hell of a time finding a place to work in civilian life. Do they think that we in the private sector will create "gay-and-lesbian-free workplaces" for those who prefer not to be in the presence of homosexuals?

Another argument is the one about how homosexuals' behavior makes them a special security risk.

My response: I can't imagine why people think gays would abandon their duty and sell out for sex more quickly than would heterosexuals. In fact, it is heterosexual men who have, more often than not, proven to be the security compromisers. The marine guards at the United States Embassy in Moscow come to mind.

Now that you have my unequivocal response to your specific question, Art, I feel impelled to tell you the long version of how I came to this point. I do it because I do not want to appear so damned self-righteous about this subject.

I must share a little personal history, perhaps more than you want to hear.

I grew up, as did most boys of my age, with very undefined feelings about "queers." Basically, my friends and I just did not understand how such people could exist, but as a result of what the bigger boys told us, our natural curiosity gave way to a kind of manufactured hostility and anger.

There was no reason for this, understand, because to our knowledge we'd never met or even seen a homosexual. But soon enough we would talk about going down to the riverfront park in Memphis to "roll some queers." This meant we intended to threaten or beat up homosexuals until they gave us their money.

My friends and I were not given to crime, but somehow, the rolling of queers seemed to have the endorsement of society. They deserved to be rolled.

Although we believed that the older boys acted out this violence against homosexuals, we never did. We just talked about it.

My next memory, also during adolescence, is of a middle-aged man who tried to pick me up at a wrestling match. He was very friendly and offered to give me a ride home, which seemed better than catching the bus. On the way to his car, something in my consciousness clicked, and I became suspicious when he tried to walk me through a dark alley not far from the riverfront. Terrified, I ran. Was he gay? I don't know.

Then, in high school, came a telephone call from Louis————, whom I had met and liked at an intracity school band function. He was direct: "Jimmy, this is Louis. How would you like a blow job?" That phrase was fairly new in those days and I didn't even know what it meant.

He explained, and I said no. "Well, at least meet me to talk about it," he said.

I agreed to meet him in a very public place. At the time, I was working nights at the newspaper with a couple of guys whom I thought to be homosexuals. One was always doing impressions of Marlene Dietrich during the coffee breaks, to the great delight of the other. They seemed not to notice the smirks of some of the other workers. They worked hard, were helpful and cooperative, and even covered my shift when I had some special event I wanted to attend.

I liked them, so I was curious enough to meet with Louis. He went into great detail about the history of homosexuality and its relationship, in his observation anyway, to great intellectual and artistic achievement. I was planning to be a musician, and I'm sure he thought the artistic connection would be very persuasive.

Suffice it to say I was not persuaded. On the other hand, these conversations and work relationships were the beginning of a change of attitude about homosexuals.

But I confess it took a long time. While I lost my adolescent hostility or any thought of doing physical harm, I still did harm in other ways. I told jokes about gay men, mimicking their walk and talk and gestures, playing into all the old stereotypes.

Long after I gave up repeating the "race" jokes of my youth, I still told the gay stories. In fact, I supported human and civil rights for African Americans, women, and people with disabilities long before I took very seriously the plight of gays and lesbians in this society.

Yet, you know something? I worked with gay men for years in the magazine business. I appreciated and profited from their talents, and I developed an enormous professional respect for them individually. All that without thinking seriously about the possibility that they were being systematically discriminated against.

The closest I came to understanding it more deeply was when I agreed to pay the moving expenses of the partner of a gay man whom I had hired from another part of the country. Despite the precedent I thought the company had established by paying moving expenses of unmarried heterosexual couples, I still caught some heat for paying the gay couple's expenses.

As for my military experience, you know I flew jet fighters in the air force for over four years, and later served in the Iowa Air National Guard, leaving finally after attaining the rank of major.

One situation comes particularly to mind. I discovered, quite by accident, that one of the pilots in our wing was *likely* a homosexual. I emphasize *likely* because once, when I was on a cross-country training flight that took me to another city, I saw him in a club with other men. Their appearance and behavior convinced me they were gay. So, assuming "birds of a feather" and all that, I ducked out of the club before he saw me.

It was a dilemma. Should I tell anyone? I knew the policy, but I also had known this man for over a year. I had flown with him; we'd had drinks in the officers' club; his behavior and his professionalism as a pilot had always impressed me as "normal" if not highly commendable.

I said nothing except to one close friend, a fairly macho man of very conservative political views. His comment was more enlightened than I think he knew: "I don't give a damn what he does in bed, as long as he doesn't try to do it to me."

In a way, Art, that kind of summed it up for me at that time.

As a pilot, I knew this: When I was flying a supersonic jet, hanging on the wing of my flight leader, at night in terrible weather, with my very survival depending on his ability, my only concern had to do with, How good a pilot is this guy? and never, I wonder what this guy's sexual orientation is?

The pilots I always worried about were those who drank a lot of booze. As for sexual exploits, there were lots. Military pilots generally are a very macho bunch, and they work overtime at it (witness the infamous "Tailhook" episode). I knew the drinking could affect our work, but I figured sex would not affect our work unless we lost a lot of sleep at it. If that's true of heterosexual sex, I assume it to be true of homosexual sex.

So, finally, here's where I come to on this subject and why I respond as I do to homosexuals in the military.

Given my professional career and my professional association with gay and lesbian people over the years, I start with a broader point of view. In my mind, military service is simply another profession, an occupation, a choice of work.

So my first question is Why should homosexuals be excluded from this particular line of work? The next question is, How can we permit our government, through its military, to *institutionalize* the discrediting and marginalizing and, indeed, the *demonizing* of any group of people in this society?

I don't want to hear the typical morality-based views, because the issue is *behavior*. All employers, including the military, have the right to demand standards of workplace behavior in any arena, including the sexual. They have the right to define "workplace" as anywhere the employee is officially representing the organization. I support that right to prescribe behavior in those settings. But employers, including the military, do not have the right to *assume* certain problematical behaviors based on superficial knowledge and prejudice.

I need not go into how the military establishments of other nations regard homosexuals or how many American homosexuals have distinguished themselves in combat. And I'll forgo stories of the Spartans, the most courageous "fighting men" the world has ever known. I'll say only this: Any reasonable person knows that homosexuals have served in the United States Armed Forces, and it is just as reasonable an assumption that many have served with heroism and distinction. Just as there are gay men and lesbians working and making their contribution to society in every occupation and profession in the country.

If we believe what we say about using all our talents and resources to compete globally, we will welcome the talents of everyone.

So what *is* all the fuss? I'm not sure I understand it completely, but I'll tell you what I think it mainly is: It is a threat to some threadbare assumptions and conventional wisdoms. If, indeed, we must begin redefining the realities of competence and service and contribution to include people who do not fit our stereotypes, then we will have taken a giant step toward erasing the last major refuge of macho paternalism in this society.

I know this prospect is discomforting to some. As for me, it would come not a moment too soon.

Love,
Dad

Understanding the Men's Movement

Dear Clare:

You have expressed a lot of doubt about the so-called men's movement. Given the media coverage, I can understand why, but I have just returned from one of the "wild man" conferences and would like to give you a report, one feminist to another, and man to woman.

I was invited to the conference to present a workshop titled "On Being a Man in Business." There were over seven hundred men at the conference, and seventy-five of them signed up for the workshop. I confess surprise that there were men from Fortune 500 companies, including AT&T, Boeing, and others.

When I was not speaking, I attended several workshops, as well as the plenary sessions. I also participated in a closing press conference.

It was, to say the least, an experience.

When I arrived at the hotel, I heard the drums. Immediately, I slipped into the cynic mode, saying to myself such things as "I wonder what happens when the drums stop?"

The first evening's session reminded me of an old-fashioned revival meeting, complete with preaching and singing and the giving of testimony. There even seemed to be those possessed by the spirit and speaking in tongues. It was a fertile medium for me to revert to my old newspaperman's sarcastic observer eye.

I guess it was the "preaching" that first changed my

attitude. The speaker, Marvin Allen, a men's movement leader in Texas, said such things as "We have to learn about *expressing* our masculinity rather than proving it."

Marvin spoke of the true power of masculinity, a power demonstrated not just in acts of physical strength, but also in acts of love and generosity—not just in expressions of invulnerability, but also in expressions of vulnerability.

It began to make a lot of sense to me, and I realized once again how, in America today, we frequently lose the meaning of our messages because we are so hung up on the medium itself.

For instance: An important message that evening involved a new definition of masculine strength. Good. But the medium was this much-publicized gathering of men, some of whom were beating on drums, some of whom were shouting *Ho* at every utterance of the speaker (reminding me of the old "Amen corner" at revival meetings), some of whom were dancing, some of whom were hugging, some of whom were made up like Native Americans, some of whom were barefoot, some of whom wore women's clothing, and so on.

In other words, there was a lot of clutter for the message to cut through. Not that the actual attendees weren't listening. They were. But the media people covering the conference could not help but be distracted by all the other stuff. Put yourself in the position of a young television reporter. Would you try to cover the "talking head" at the podium, or would you be getting good footage of all those kooky guys?

I believe there were two or three young men dressed

like women. Interestingly, their message was a protest against rape and the abuse of women. The message, of course, was lost in the medium they chose. Not only that, the TV cameras spent a lot of time with those young men, ignoring the 698 other men.

Forgive me if this letter is beginning to sound as if it were written by the late Marshall McLuhan. I'm not trying to steal his stuff, only trying to explain why your impressions of the men's movement cannot possibly reflect the truth of the movement, because that truth becomes obfuscated by our fascination with some of the more visible aspects of the movement.

I certainly was no different, sarcastic as I was in my first impressions.

In the individual workshops, there were groups whose members crawled on the floor, bumping into one another, groaning and carrying on in unusual if not strange ways. There were others in which men admitted their disappointments, their deep hurts and grief, and allowed themselves to just weep, some for the first time, I suspect.

The uninvolved or uninitiated observer could not be blamed for missing the point and reporting only the surface events. Yet it did not require a major commitment of time or of simply paying attention to understand that something very important was going on. Important for both men and women.

How can I say it without trivializing it or without making it so tedious you'll put this letter aside for another day? Maybe it is as simple as this: The men at this conference were learning not about how to feel, but about how to recognize their feelings for what they are and about how to express those feelings. Many of the men were in the first stage of this development, which means they were overdoing it, were letting go completely, and in so doing, were experiencing perhaps their first taste of emotional "freedom."

Next, the men at this conference were learning that they did not have to live their lives in the image of the great macho man whose strength is expressed only physically and who may, by hiding everything behind that macho image, really be emotionally disabled. And last, these men were learning, some of them for the first time, how to talk to one another about things other than sex, sports, politics, and business.

I know this sounds like emotional baby steps to you, and probably to most other women, but try to recognize its importance, and try to give these men their due. At least they're trying.

As for the notion of "men's movement," I'm not sure there is one. There's a lot of talk about it, to be sure, but it seems to me that movements are characterized by an agenda of action to which other elements of society—government, business, education, and so on—are expected to respond.

There were men at this conference who represented various elements of what is considered the men's movement: the mythopoetic "movement," the "profeminists," some "antifeminists," and various "warrior" groups. And yet, in asking men to define the movement for me, I generally received the same answer, something about feelings and expressing them, and inner growth and recovery, and rediscovering the masculine, and so on.

When I asked, "What is your list of demands?" the answers had to do with other people's expectations of "manhood" and how that should change.

"No laws to pass?"

"No."

"No policy changes in Fortune 500 companies?"

"No, well, at least not institutionally."

"You mean the people within those institutions must change their attitudes and expectations of men or manhood or masculinity?"

"Yes."

My conclusion is that there may be a men's movement, but I could not find it at that conference. What I could find were seven hundred men trying their damnedest to learn more about themselves and one another, and to figure out ways to express that in a world often hostile to any tampering with the conventional definitions of "masculinity."

The above is not exactly a slogan to fit on a banner to carry in a march on Washington (as one participant noted), but this may well be some of the most important and powerful man stuff in the country right now.

If, as Marvin Allen says, it leads to men understanding that there is an appropriate expression of masculine power in participating in those acts of love and tenderness so often described as "feminine," such as taking care of children, working with underprivileged people, showing a troubled fellow employee that you care, treating your employees with compassion and caring, working with the elderly, or, simply, crying with a friend in a time of tragedy—then I don't care what we call it.

But let's stop calling it a lot of what we've heard it called by those who fear or ridicule or trivialize it.

Or to put it another way, Clare, how about cutting us men a little slack? We're trying harder these days.

With love,
Dad

Part Three

Community and Friendship

A Cry of Frustration

I have spent most of my adult life as a defender of, and advocate for, the First Amendment. I believe it has been one of the keys to the greatness of this country, and I believe that, without the First Amendment's guarantees, not only would we be worse off, but America as we know it would not even exist today.

So it is particularly troubling to me that I now feel our popular culture has greatly abused and exploited the right of free speech, and it is particularly difficult to frame my own views in a way that does not seem to be calling for censorship, to which I am unalterably opposed.

I also recoil from the self-righteousness associated with those who call for more "responsibility" on the part of pop culture heroes.

But somewhere in there, somewhere between "responsibility," "common sense," and "stewardship of our culture" is a subject for the serious consideration of businesspeople.

It seems a matter of obvious and very common sense to me that we can so exploit any right that we end up destroying it altogether.

Lest you think I'm talking about hard-core pornography, let me quickly say I am moved to these thoughts by the things to which Ronald (age nine and with autism) is exposed: closely supervised television and closely supervised movies.

Case in point: *Batman Returns.* Ronald had seen the first *Batman,* which was bad enough. I hoped only that he could perceive that the violence was cartoon-y, thus relatively harmless. I hoped that same thing, incidentally, in the *Home Alone* movies, both of which stress violence—rather than going to the authorities—as a child's appropriate expression of self-sufficiency.

Now comes *Batman Returns*. It was plotless, weird, gratuitously and pointlessly violent, gratuitously and pointlessly sexual, and, as the kids would say, gross. It was not even a morality tale. It was the worst kind of pyrotechnic pandering to the absolutely sickest kinds of taste (dubious word). The critics who called it "just good fun" have very distorted notions of fun. I was offended, but there was no explaining this crap to Ronald. To those who say, "You could have just left in the middle," I answer, "Just try to drag a normal nine-year-old out of a movie, much less one with autism."

Furthermore, the hype of this film was greatly aided and abetted by the toy companies and fast-food companies which jumped on the promotional bandwagon and, in so doing, put their own reputations and imprimatur on the movie. Everything about the public image of the project said *family entertainment.*

Another "family" film promoted and advertised specifically to children was *Kindergarten Cop,* the theme of which was the stalking and kidnapping of a young boy. This movie, with its graphically violent ending, terrified kids.

Beyond a few Disney films, the movie marketplace is a wasteland for young children (not to mention for adults, but that is another subject). Lest we praise Disney too quickly, however, let's not forget *The Hand That Rocks the Cradle,* which Michael Eisner described last year in a *New Yorker* article as "a silly movie, a fun movie." Some fun.

Television is another story. Fortunately, Sally and I can and do control access to the TV. Occasionally, I watch one of the top-rated shows just to know what people are watching. Mostly, it's junk. A lot of it is sex, violence, the darkest side of society. Most of the rest of it borders on silliness. Even the comedy writers don't seem to think they can score a laugh without resorting to "pee-pee doo-doo" jokes.

Need I talk about pop music and some of its messages?

Part of my concern, of course, is the access children have to this material, but I also feel that a lot of this stuff begins to greatly distort our adult perceptions of reality, rather than simply reflecting reality.

I worry also about adolescents and teenagers and the ever-greater pressures they face. In the most emotionally delicate (and volatile) years of their lives, they are also our most technologically savvy generation ever, the result of which is that they are bombarded with an endless stream of images, both visual and auditory. A very high proportion of the images stress two messages:

1. Sex exists unto itself as a low-common-denominator activity which is more of a sport than it is a physical expression of affection, love, and attachment.

2. Problems are to be eliminated and not solved, and frequently, the process of elimination involves violence to other people.

The pop culture gives these young people no other choices. Part of the issue is indeed choice. Is the offering of more life-affirming and love-affirming material to be left only in the hands of specifically sectarian religionists? I hope not, and my friends in the popular arts had better join me in that hope.

I know I'm already beginning to sound like the Reverend Mr. Wildmon of Tupelo, Mississippi, who raves about this sort of thing. But there's a difference. I believe he would gladly abrogate the First Amendment to get rid of the material that offends him. I would not.

So what do I want?

Speaking as a businessman, I'd like to see the businesses that profit from these various pop culture enterprises exercise more common sense and restraint. To my mind, it is no longer good enough to excuse this material on the basis of artistic freedom when the motivations clearly are not artistic.

My observation, based on years of trying to get various businesses and businesspeople to join in efforts to support the First Amendment, is that most of them don't give a damn about those causes until their businesses are threatened, then they wrap the First Amendment around themselves as if it were the flag and the Ten Commandments combined.

I can't respect those defenders of the First Amendment who refuse to practice good, old-fashioned judgment about what they put into the marketplace, claiming that it is okay to sing or say or show anything—no matter how violent or hateful or destructive—as long as enough people will pay money for it. There is a hypocrisy there somewhere, or at the very least, there is an astonishing ignorance about what happens when institutions abdicate the responsibility of judging their activities in the context of what is good for society.

I know there can be a multitude of transgressions, from censorship to manipulation, hiding behind the facade of "responsible judgment" and "what is good for society." Yet, without institutions overcoming their perceived need for short-term gains, economic or otherwise, and trying to establish, or reestablish, their moral authority in an attempt to help lead a return to civility, the job will be left—by abdication—to the self-appointed morality police.

But I do not claim that it's easy. History is filled with episodes of editors, publishers, or producers who wrongly would not provide the medium for a truly wonderful book, play, or film because they judged its content to be offensive or otherwise undesirable.

I admit that is a risk, but I am confident that these dilemmas will yield to good judgment, and I am confident that businesspeople can come up with an open process for arriving at those judgments. For if they don't, then I fear they will just be setting themselves up for the kind of dramatic "family values" backlash that will result in governmental attempts to restrain them—regardless of who is sitting in the White House.

And these businesspeople should not kid themselves into thinking that it is only religious fundamentalists who care about family values and who care about the content of what their children are exposed to. I have read interviews with and articles by Hollywood executives who, in effect, claim that the critics are trying to require movies to adhere to the moral criteria of a perfect society.

My only response is, "Wake up, folks! Not many people think we are going to achieve a perfect society. This cry is from people scared by a quite imperfect society, a society filled with homicide, suicide, addiction, unwanted pregnancies, abused spouses and children, unwanted and abandoned children, with an increasing level of violence informing all these conditions."

I hear these concerns expressed among the most open and politically liberal people I know. I believe a demand to "do something" is growing toward a critical mass.

Meanwhile, as I hope for a new examination of corporate responsibility in this arena, I also will continue to do my damnedest to support these companies' right to produce or publish or record anything, including the offensive, destructive, and irresponsible junk.

But the battle is increasingly uphill.

Getting Beyond the Babble

Dear Clare:

Every columnist in America has written his or her version of the "politically correct" movement, such as it is, and its impact on free speech. I hate to disappoint you, but I have nothing to add to those arguments.

I will observe only that the imposition of any one point of view is essentially destructive to this society, regardless of the point of view and regardless of the setting. This attitude, of course, doesn't necessarily make me popular even among those with whose liberal viewpoints I usually agree. (You'll recall that, years ago, I used to tell you that a liberal was someone who loved humankind but couldn't much stand folks, and a conservative was someone who wanted everyone who disagreed with him to have the unrestricted freedom and liberty to leave the country.)

I believe the current situation boils down to this: Virtually everybody in the society seems spring-loaded to their righteous indignation. It is their first response to anyone or any viewpoint that does not suit them.

The situation is exacerbated by the fact that no one truly listens to the other viewpoint. They just shout louder and louder, presumably in the belief that volume is better than persuasion.

What better example than the current television shows hosted by Donahue and Oprah and Geraldo and others, as well as those Washington commentary shows like *Crossfire* and *The McLaughlin Group*? The mode of communication on all these programs is heated confrontation and shouting.

We are close to becoming the fabled Tower of Babel, not speaking in separate languages but splitting our one language into many self-protective parts. We code our language for our own group, inserting such an obscure set of value-loaded and meaning-loaded words and phrases that only our own group can understand what we are *really* saying (if you know what I mean).

All of this—the unrelenting viewpoints, the shouting, the code words—are antithetical to the direction in which we must go if the country is truly to capitalize on what we grandly call the strength of our diversity.

Don't get me wrong. I believe in the strength of our diversity, but I also believe there is a lot of big talk about diversity by people who don't really understand the true meaning of what they're talking about.

For instance, when executives of companies state a goal of diversifying the work force, they generally mean achieving more integration of racial and ethnic groups, and achieving more gender balance. But I don't believe they mean acceptance and tolerance of the cultural differences inherent in that diversification. And I believe that, while they expect those other racial and ethnic groups to look different, they expect them to act and think "like everyone else," which of course defeats the very purpose of diversification.

It ain't going to happen like that, just as it ain't going to happen in America that we all believe the same things on any subject, including the definition of patriotism.

We never have and we never will.

But I do believe that we are now less civil than we were, less tolerant, less accepting, and less understanding; we have forgotten that as citizens, we are not called upon to approve of one another, but only to accept one another.

Without the civility of acceptance versus the riotous babble of disapproval, dear Clare, it won't matter much longer who is or isn't "politically correct."

With apologies for sounding like your doomsday dad,

Dad

A Graduation Gift

Dear Sue:

In addition to the cash which I know a graduate always needs, I want to give you something more substantial. In a way, what follows this letter is a bit of family history which I hope you will reflect upon from time to time; in another way, it is my way of giving you the most valuable advice I can offer.

I'm sure you're wondering, "Why this particular poem?"

Surely, as you read it, you may also think, "So what? What does this little poem about our now-deceased dirt-farmer relative in Mississippi have to do with me as I start out for the difficult world?"

Another question I might add to yours is, What in the world difference does it make anyway, all that attention to how those routine everyday chores were done? Does it really matter? Isn't the point just to get the clothes pressed, the garden plowed, the knives sharpened, the fire started, the apple peeled, and then get on with life?

Ah, yes. Get on with life. I remember so well how anxious I was to get on with life as I graduated. But my ambitions were rather limited. By all conventional definitions, I am a person of accomplishment, so it will surprise you to know just exactly what my ambitions were while I was in college. They were simple: work as a newspaperman and make fifty dollars a week.

That's it.

I visit college classes and tell this to students and they

are astounded. What? No life plan? No goals? No time-table for position and income?

Well, yes, I had a life plan and a goal: be a newspa-perman and make fifty dollars a week.

So how did I get to where I am, you may ask.

I wish I could say for certain, but I am not sure. I know that part of it was luck, being in the right place at the right time. But how did I know what to do in that right place at the right time?

I've asked myself that question many times. Most of the answer, I think, is based on some pretty old-fashioned stuff, though *I certainly did not realize it at the time.*

Now when students and new employees ask me for advice, I tell them what I believe will work and what has worked for me and for every person of accomplishment I know. Concentrate on the very thing you are to do *before* you do it, concentrate on it *while* you are doing it, then work harder than anyone ever expects you to. More and more companies are becoming meritocracies in which hard work and real accomplishment are rewarded, rather than politics and personal maneuvering.

This brings me back to the fire and the laundry and the apple peel of my poem.

All those little chores. How important was it to do them with such loving attention to how they are done? Just this: Whatever you set yourself to do in this life, Sue, it makes the *greatest difference imaginable* that you do it with an abiding sense of excellence. Not just excellence in the result, but excellence in the doing, the process, the effort.

The quality of the effort is crucial to you and to your

growth; in fact, the quality of your effort transcends even the finished quality of whatever you are doing.

As you strive for that excellence and quality in everything, please understand that there are many *results* that you will not be able to control. Understand that other factors, other influences can affect the results you achieve. Who knows what those factors will be? There may be a problem with the economy. There may be a problem with the availability of resources. There may be a problem with deadlines or with the contribution of another person.

Please abandon whatever notions you have about how much control you will have over the results you achieve in life.

And know this: The only thing you *can* control, the only thing you can *always* bring excellence to, the only thing you can grow from and feel fulfilled by and feel ennobled by and ultimately be rewarded by is the quality of your own effort.

Oh, I know plenty of lives filled with rationalization, with the belief that "I'll just whip through this little job and save my good stuff for the more important job."

But remember this: The only important job you will ever have is the one you are doing. This job. Today. Right now.

I know how difficult it is and will be. I know we must have vision, we must look ahead and set goals and plan for our future. This is as it should be. But my message is not one of "live for today and never think about tomorrow." To the contrary, my message is, "Assure yourself of success and happiness tomorrow, and assure that your vision will be fulfilled by concentrating on the excellence of your efforts today."

After all, our lives are but an accumulation of the things we have done, in our work and in our play and in our relationships. My prayer for you, Sue, is that your life may be an accumulation of days and years of things every bit as important and significant as fires well made, hogs well fed, and apple peels stretching halfway to the floor.

In other words, I pray for you a whole lifetime of things—big and small—done right.

> With love and congratulations,
> Uncle Jim

THINGS DONE RIGHT

I.

Now there are ruts in the floor
where Aunt Callie rocks with a morning cup of coffee
and warms her feet at a gas heater
whose black pipe shoots into the old chimney
where the fireplace had been.

But back when the ruts were young,
the first sounds of morning were ashes being stirred,
the thump of fresh logs,
the pop of pine kindling in the cook stove,
the quiet talk of the grownups,
and the radio with its thin and fuzzy hillbilly music.
  How many biscuits can you eat
  this mornin' this mornin'
and the weather reports Uncle Vee always turned up.
We'd hear him walk to the door
and know he was looking at the sky.
  Don't care what the weather man says
  gonna rain this afternoon
Then the radio would go down
and Aunt Callie and Uncle Vee would have their quiet time
and talk about the day
and he would say where he planned to work
and she would talk about washing or canning
or sewing or working the garden,
and they would decide what we children would do.

We'd hear the hiss of something frying
and wonder what it was before we could smell it,
salt meat or bacon or maybe country ham.
   Better call those chirrun
   biscuits goin' in
And the smells settling into the whole house,
all the way under the covers
would help us wake up.

II.

Even in the hot of July
the cook stove was fired
and Aunt Callie baked biscuits every meal
using her big wooden dough bowl of flour
and pinching in lard and squeezing in buttermilk,
working it with her hands
then lifting the dough and rolling it out,
cutting the biscuits with a baking powder can.

And there might be fried pies
sealed with a fork dipped in water
and pressed evenly along a crescent edge,
or a fruit pie with a tall crust
scalloped by the quick and perfect twists
of a buttered thumb and forefinger.
Between meals Aunt Callie kept the stove hot
simmering a slow pot of string beans and salt meat,
boiling water for dishes,
heating irons on the day after washday.
How she would sweat in her loose wash dress,

ironing everything from the clothesline,
sprinkling with her hand dripping from a pan of water,
working fast before her iron cooled down,
licking her finger and sizzling it against the iron
to check its hotness
as it sat on an old coffee-can lid
at the end of the ironing board.
And leaving no piece of cloth untouched,
dish towels, sheets, tablecloths, and washrags,
overalls and work shirts
which would be sweat wet and wrinkled in five minutes,
and folding everything on shelves and in drawers
as if they would never be touched
but be looked at and admired
and passed on
by some work clothes inspector.

On other days she churned,
humming hymns to the wet rhythm of the dasher,
the kitchen filled with bowls and buckets of milk,
clabber or blue John or buttermilk,
with cheesecloth keeping out the flies.

III.

And Uncle Vee was the same,
the way he hitched his mule
and plowed his garden,
geeing and hawing up and down the rows,
the way he put in his potatoes and onion sets,
then unhitched the mule and fed and watered him,

the way he measured two double handfuls of shorts
for each hog and mixed it with slop from the table
as if the hogs might not eat it done wrong.

And in the evening after supper,
he laid a fire with pine knots and split wood
so it burned with one match
and never had to be stoked a second time,
then sat with a cup of coffee
and always worked on something,
maybe patching a stew pan with screws and a washer
or rigging a trotline or cleaning his double barrel
or sharpening his barlow knife,
spitting on a whetrock
and drawing the blade toward him and away
and testing its sharpness against the hairs on his arm.
    Most dangerous things in the world, boys,
     is a dull knife
     Cut you faster'n a sharp one
And while Aunt Callie snapped peas or shelled butterbeans,
he would peel an apple,
putting his barlow to it and turning the apple
so the peel came in one long spiral
stretching halfway to the floor.
    You ain't peeled an apple
     till you can do that, boys
And when we tried it,
then and much, much later,
the peel always broke and fell
and the apple never tasted the same.

The Hard Work of Community

There has been a lot of talk in the past several years about the breakdown of our cities. What I believe has broken down is not the cities, but the communities within the cities. And those communities need to be recreated. In other words, we may be living in the same country or area or city but we are not living *in community* with one another.

But creating a community is difficult.

I'm not talking about the act of laying out a town or city, physically building it with bricks and mortar and with streets and utilities, then adding the institutions of government, church, education, and business. Creating a community has little to do with construction or, for that matter, with institutions.

In fact, it seems clear that with all our institutions and with all our technology, we as people are becoming more and not less fragmented and alienated from one another.

And this comes at a time when major social research shows that one of the most dominant attitudes people are expressing now is the need for community and connection.

When people say "community and connection," what do you suppose they are thinking? What are they longing for? What do you believe they are missing?

Unfortunately, I think most people are thinking about and longing for and missing a notion of community that rarely existed. Consider, for instance, the community portrayed in the following, one of my most popular poems.

DEATH IN THE FAMILY

I.

People hug us and cry
and pray we'll be strong
and know we'll see her again someday.
And we nod and they pat and rub,
reassuring her to heaven.
   She's with Jesus now,
   no suffering where she is.
Then sit on hard benches and sing
of precious memories how they linger
and farther along we'll understand it.
   Cheer up my brother,
   we're not forgotten. . . .
The preacher studies his Bible and stares at the ceiling
and the song leader in his blue funeral suit sweats
and strokes the air
with a callused hand.
   We'll understand it
   all bye and bye. . . .
And powdered and rosy-cheeked
Miss Anne sleeps in an open coffin,
the children standing tiptoe to see through the flowers
but scared to go near and drawing back when lifted.
And the choir brings a Balm in Gilead
and a Roll Is Called Up Yonder,
   When the trumpet of the Lord shall sound
   and time shall be no more . . .

and big men shake heads white at the hat line
while women weep and flutter air with palm leaf fans.
And later we stand amidst the stones
by the mound of red clay,
our eyes wet against the sun
and listen to preachers and mockingbirds
and the 23rd Psalm.

II.

Men stand uneasy in ties
and nod their hats to ladies
and kick gravel with shoes too tight
and talk about life.
   Nobody no better'n Miss Anne,
   No sir,
   No sir.
Smoking Bull Durhams around the porch,
shaking their heads to agree,
and sucking wind through their teeth,
   Never let you go thirsty,
   bring a jugga tea to the field
   ever day
they open doors for us and look at the ground
as if by not seeing our faces they become invisible.
There are not enough chores,
so three draw well water
and two get the mail
and four feed the dogs
and the rest chop wood
and wish for something to say.

178

Lester broke his arm one time
and Miss Anne plowed that mule
like a man,
put in the whole crop.
And they talk of crops and plowing,
of rain and sun and flood and drought,
the seasons passing in memory
marking changes in years and lives
that men remember at times
when there's nothing to say.

III.

Ladies come with sad faces
and baskets of sweets—
teacakes, pecan pies, puddings, memories—
and we choose and they serve,
telling stories and God-blessing the children,
I declare that Miss Anne
was the sweetest Christian person
in the world
saying all the things to be said,
doing all the things to be done,
like orderly spirits,
freshening beds from the grieving night,
poking up fires gone cold,
filling the table and sideboard
then gathering there to urge and cajole
as if the dead rest easier on our full stomachs.
Lord how Miss Anne would have loved that country ham.
No sadness so great it cannot be fed away

by the insistent spirits.
  That banana cake is her very own recipe.
  I remember how she loved my spoon bread.
  She canned the berries in this cobbler.
And suddenly we are transformed
and eat and smile and thank you,
and the ladies nod and know they have done well again
in time of need,
and the little girls watch and learn.
And we forget the early spring cemetery
and the church with precious memories,
and farther along we do understand it,
the payments and repayments
of all the ladies that were and are
and we pray ever will be. Amen.

The poem you've just read describes a church congregation and a community of love and ritual and family connections which seem to touch what many people have experienced, particularly in small towns and rural areas. Readers of my first book, *Nights Under a Tin Roof*, in which the poem appeared, have written to tell me that they "wish life could be like that again."

But I confess to you that my childhood view of those days, if applied to the community as a whole, was very much distorted. Don't misunderstand. I believe deeply in those rituals of community and in their ability to bring us close to one another, and I say nothing to detract from, or denigrate in any way, that nurturing experience in my life.

On the other hand, it is false to say that I wrote about a whole community. The scene from my poem takes place in Mississippi, and I can assure you that there were no black faces in that church. Black folks may have been standing outside, listening through the open windows, but they were not inside.

And some of the people inside were not really *included*. There were disabled people left to their own devices most of the time, living alone, having little opportunity for education or work.

There were alcoholics who were not treated but simply laughed at. There were women and children who had been abused, though no one talked about those things in those days. And of course, there were simply the people at the bottom of the economic barrel who, if they weren't black, probably were called "poor white trash."

In other words, there were plenty of people who did

not feel part of the community I wrote about so lovingly, and I suggest that those people did not feel so lovingly about the same time and place, regardless of my childhood impressions.

Now, as an adult, I realize there can be no real community unless *all* people can feel a part of it. Please don't think me naive. I know that not everyone will participate. I wish only that everyone might have the opportunity to do so.

As M. Scott Peck, author of *The Different Drum: Community-Making and Peace*, says:

> The great enemy of community is exclusivity. Groups that exclude others are . . . actually bastions against community. . . .
>
> There is a vast difference between a group and a community. Groups value sameness while communities value individuality. Groups want everyone to be strong, achieving up to a certain standard. Communities recognize that some are weak and can never achieve certain standards, then communities honor the weak, respect their viewpoint, and realize that the strong, if indeed they have a deep sense of community, are called to help the weak.

Pretty lofty stuff, huh?

Maybe, but this is the stuff we have to involve ourselves in if we are to solve our problems and become the community we must become.

It would be much easier for all of us to draw into ourselves, to emphasize the negative aspects of our differences, and to wait for someone else to do the work of community, hoping we can join later.

I admit there are plenty of days when our problems seem insurmountable, and there are days when I despair.

But I do believe fundamentally that miracles happen when we respect one another for what we are and for what we can contribute, though we may not look or behave or even be able to contribute the same as someone else.

I have tried in my career as a business manager to dispel some of the false conventional wisdoms and have tried to help people realize that the workplace is indeed a community, and that it is part of the manager's job to build that community.

This doesn't set well with a lot of managers, because most of us worked so hard during our careers to promulgate the myth that everyone in our department or on our team is an outstanding performer. This meant, of course, no tolerance for those who did not "perform," or contribute, according to our preconceptions.

I believe that insecure people, including managers (and I mean managers at the very top of companies), tend to make others over in their own image—or they surround themselves with people who think similarly.

They mistake uniformity for unity.

The result is exclusivity. I like to tell managers and employees, "Look, we don't have to love one another, we don't even have to like one another, and we certainly don't have to approve of one another all the time.

"But we do have to care about one another. We have to realize that what we do here, we do together, and we cannot succeed unless we do it together. We have to realize that we must depend on one another. There is no other way.

"That means caring and acceptance and support, even though you might never want to see the other person outside of this workplace."

I believe these principles apply to any community: city, town, church, school, or workplace. This means giving of our time and effort, working together, building coalitions, and developing, organizing, and focusing both institutional and personal resources.

This means believing enough in the positive power of community that even in our disagreements we always try to look for what is good and what is possible in one another.

THE SUMMER OF 1992

In my flowers, an unusual visitor,
a goldfinch eating seeds
from a fading stand of coreopsis,
gold and black on gold and black.

Last month, a storm
blew my young corn to the ground.
Now the stalks are tasseling
but there are no silks
and without them the pollen
is just another broken promise.

In the newspaper, a famine
in Somalia and killing in Yugoslavia
and South Africa and Uzbekistan,
places where hope seems to bear no fruit
after a season of such expectation.

This morning, I cut leaves and suckers
from the tomatoes which
for no reason I understand
have overgrown with foliage
and now need a new surge of life
and sunshine before it is too late.

It has been a strange summer.
All the sure signs are unreliable.
Everything is late in ripening.
There seems nothing to do,
yet waiting is not enough.

THE EVIDENCE

(For Mark W. Bennett, U.S. Magistrate Judge,
on the occasion of his swearing in)

Learned people speak learned words,
crowding sentences with jargon and acronym,
the assembled evidence
of a path taken toward this time and place.

I come with a different testimony,
not of law but of love,
of a parallel path
toward this same time and place.

Yet I sit in this courtroom with no hard evidence,
no sworn statements,
no pleadings,
no depositions.
All the evidence is soft,
but, may it please the court,
that is the power of it.

Who Really Pays
Corporate Taxes?

Dear Sue:

So you think corporations should pay more taxes. I'm not surprised, and you can take comfort in that opinion, because a lot of people agree with you.

But I'm not one of them. In fact, I'm not sure that in the grand scheme of things we are well served by corporations paying taxes at all.

It's too late to turn back the clock on that one, of course, and it could be that because corporations receive special recognition under the law, they *should* pay some share of taxes. But understand this reality: Corporations don't pay any taxes when all is said and done. The corporation's customers pay the taxes in the form of prices. If corporations pay more taxes, prices go up to cover the cost of the taxes.

Some observers believe that taxing corporations has advantages beyond just the tax revenue collection. They point out that because corporations (and other companies) do pay taxes, the government is able to encourage certain investment or employment policies by providing tax incentives or disincentives according to what it wants the companies to do.

Want companies to invest more in plant and equipment? Provide an investment tax credit or some other such device. Want companies to hold on to assets for a certain minimum period of time before selling? Have a special capital gains tax rate, then tie it to that minimum time period. In other words, if you sell the assets before the minimum time, you pay a higher tax rate.

So I might concede that tax policy is a good way to exert influence over the actions of companies, in order to direct them for the greater social good. (Unfortunately, the definition of the greater social good changes as administrations change.) But it is also true that regardless of tax policy, the customer ends up paying.

And that's the way it is supposed to work in this system. A company adds up all its costs, matches them to revenues, and with good planning, management, and a little luck, takes in more money than it pays out, resulting in a profit. If the costs go up, the revenues must go up, which means, usually, that prices must go up.

So agitate for higher corporate taxes, if you wish, but understand that if your favorite automobile company pays higher taxes, you'll pay more for the car.

Of course, it's more complicated than that, but this is a pretty good common-sense way to think about how our system works.

Love,
Uncle Jim

Bringing Public Schools
and Business Together

A compelling question for our society is, How can business and the public schools work together better?

In these days of tight budgets and more limited resources, it seems to have become fashionable for businesspeople to criticize educators for consuming vast quantities of public money while turning out a "product" of diminishing quality. They point to test scores and achievement levels, then compare our graduates—always unfavorably—to the graduates in our "competitor" countries. They complain that American companies will not be able to compete globally unless the schools turn out an educated and prepared work force.

In response, educators have hunkered down defensively, pointing out that businesspeople just don't understand the pressures on schools these days: discipline problems, federal and state legislative mandates, increased criticism from all parts of the political spectrum, and public expectations that the schools should do everything—such as prevent AIDS and other sexually transmitted diseases, drug use, and teenage pregnancy—in addition to educating our young people and preparing them to participate fully in society.

There are arguments on both sides, but clearly, the answers do not lie in more arguments. I believe it is fair to say we have the problems defined and surrounded, and now must move toward finding the solutions. And I believe we must begin with joint efforts between business and educators to make our public schools work better for everyone. This will require an attitude of partnership, one that goes beyond the informal partnerships and sponsorships now existing between some schools and businesses locally.

As in any partnership, each partner has special needs. Certainly, in this day and age, the schools are in great need of support by business. It is only in business's best interest to support the schools, to actively work toward programs and activities that will not only educate and socialize young people generally, but will prepare them specifically for the world of work.

Business needs to allocate resources—time, money, and people to work with—and in schools, to provide educators and students the direct experience of thinking and working in a business context. Business must open its doors to both students and faculty intern and mentoring programs. And business must do it with a sincere commitment, not just as some sort of half hearted and faint-hearted part of its magnanimous "community relations" program. Furthermore, business people must stop their typical knee-jerk reaction against spending money for better education.

I shall not belabor the need for improved education, for a well-trained work force to help business compete globally. You've heard all that. It's important. And it's true.

On the other side, business deserves to have the education community be responsive to business's future needs, and to align many of the educational programs and courses of study *specifically* toward the needs of business.

Also, business deserves for the schools to take seriously the teaching about our economic system and its positive contributions, not only to economic growth but to social growth.

I believe that educators must try to understand more fully the pressures of business; I believe educators must be attentive to recognizing, identifying, and defining the greater social roles of business and how those roles are fulfilled; and I believe educators must do what they can to break down some of the misleading and destructive stereotypes about business and businesspeople. It's a bum rap. Those of us in business know there are charlatans, fools, and crooks in business, but we know that they are the minority by far and that most businesspeople are hard-working, honest, forthright, caring, and concerned citizens.

I'd like to see the schools present an offsetting, balancing story to the one in the popular media, including movies and television which generally lead our young people to believe that business is the breeding ground of greed, avarice, and mendacity. I believe there is a *community* responsibility of educators to offset some of that propaganda.

Both partners in this partnership, schools and business, must help and support each other in efforts and initiatives that may not appear *directly* beneficial to either of them, particularly economically, and which may be less beneficial to themselves than to the community at large.

In our headlong drive to bring quantifiable evaluation to education, we must not overlook a great truth: that the *process of education itself* has value to individual students and to society, value that may not be measurable in a numerical way.

As we try to develop educational programs in the vital effort to support business in its need to be globally competitive, and as we try to develop ways for business to support education as an expression of its own enlightened self-interest, I think it is important for both partners to realize this: *Not every student will contribute to the same extent, and not every course of study will help global competitiveness.*

We will have slow learners and children with disabilities who will have to do the best they can and who must be given the opportunity to contribute as best they can and to the extent that they can in our society, whether it helps global competitiveness or not; plus, we will have those students who want to paint or write or dance or sculpt or play an instrument or simply ponder the great mysteries of life.

Without these slow learners and underachievers and people with disabilities; without the artists and poets and actors; without the philosophers and theologians; without the players of sport whose only sense of global competitiveness is the Olympics; in other words, without all those people who are *not* going to enter our businesses or our work forces and become a direct part of the business-driven economic system, our communities and our society would be greatly diminished.

We would, in fact, be spiritually impoverished.

So, as we work toward a partnership between business and the schools, we must remember that there is always another partner in the mix. And remember that the major partners always have an abiding and binding responsibility not only to see to the growth and welfare of one another, but also to use that synergy which a good partnership always produces to reach out and be a partner to the whole community.

Defining the
Really Good Things in Life

Dear Sue:

I guess I'm turning into a blubbering old fool. I cry at the drop of a hat, and don't even know why.

Several times during your high school production of *The Music Man* last week, I found myself sitting there in pure delight; at the same time, I was choking back tears.

Perhaps it was the innocence of the musical itself, of course, but also of you and your friends. Oh, I know, I know. You'd not describe your friends, yourself, and other teenagers as "innocent" these days. You're all informed about sex and drugs, some of you having already done both, and you know about AIDS, and you have been exposed to an increasingly graphic treatment in the media of all of society's most violent and depraved inclinations.

But there is an innocence in getting up on that stage and singing and dancing your heads off, an innocence born of simply giving it your best. Take my word for it.

Perhaps all my sentimentality has something to do with a delayed recognition of the fragility of those simple things that make up so much of what is good in life. I recognize, too, that I spent too much of my life ignoring those pleasures, looking instead for the rewards that come with career and money.

This is an old story, and I certainly don't believe that this letter will add significantly to all the other writings and lectures you'll hear on this subject as you make your own life's journey.

Also, I am not naive enough to try to dissuade you from building a successful career, by the conventional definitions of society, or from trying to enjoy your success through money and material rewards. And don't worry. I'm not about to break into that old song, "The Best Things in Life Are Free."

Because they're not. Everything "costs," in that everything requires some kind of commitment. Sometimes it's money, sometimes it's time, sometimes it's simply the energy to pay attention and respond to the people around you.

And I include especially the people with whom you will work. Just as you had to make some special bond with your fellow cast members of *The Music Man*, so will you have to make a special bond with your fellow workers, regardless of the work, the place, or the people.

Just as you had conflict with fellow cast members, with you jealous of some of them and some of them jealous of you, with the irritations and blow-ups, so will you have those same conflicts with your fellow workers. And just as, at the cast party, amidst the tears and laughter and enormous sense of accomplishment, you felt closer to your fellow cast members in that time and place than to any other group of people at any other time—almost like family—so will you have that kind of joy with your fellow workers.

I have felt all these emotions and connections at work. I have felt at one with my colleagues, even when there were times of conflict and disagreement. And the occasions don't have to be monumental. It happens in little ways every day as we, each in his or her own job, create some piece of the larger work, sometimes not even realizing what the outcome of all our efforts will be.

There are those times when the outcomes are disappointing. But there are also those times when the outcomes are more than we ever could have hoped for.

Imagine that: people working together in an office or in a department store or in an assembly plant, each doing a piece of something, then being able to see that some thing, bigger than life and a result of their own community effort, and realizing that they did it together, not only *with* one another but *because* of one another.

That realization is one of those simple, fragile things that make up what is good in life. It is difficult to remain aware of these experiences and it becomes more difficult as time goes on, because the more successful you are, and often, the more money you make, the more difficult it is to recognize these little transcendent moments when they happen.

But remain open to the possibilities throughout your career and life. When the moments come, rejoice in them just as you did when the curtain went down on *The Music Man*.

And, might I also add, if the tears feel like flowing, don't waste time trying to choke them back.

Love,
Uncle Jim

ON THE CONCORDE

3/26/90 N.Y.–Paris

Thirty years ago
when few had done it
and doing it was something rare,
we wore in our lapels
the emblem of the Machbusters' Club,
that loose collection of fighter pilots
who in straight-down dives
had entered the exclusive world
beyond the speed of sound.
We swaggered,
we of the bent wing airplanes,
the Sabre jet boys,
the ones with caps worn low
on the bridge of our nose,
the ones with top buttons unbuttoned,
uniforms no longer suited for the new domain.

How primitive it seems,
sitting now in a business suit,
with my wife who at mach one point seven oh,
is looking at a map of Paris,
who did not notice when we slipped
through what was once called

the barrier.
And I think, for the first time
in three decades,
"I'm going the fastest I've ever gone,"
then close my eyes for a nap.

ON HEARING THE UKRAINIAN CHILDREN SING IN CHURCH

Des Moines, Iowa, January 24, 1993

Twenty years before these children were born,
I fought the Cold War
at a small air base in Germany
where I spent the days studying maps,
checking the plane and the bomb,
then practicing,
practicing in my head,
always ready,
even eager,
for the call,
and where I spent the nights dressed
in everything but my boots,
waiting for the siren
that would send me running
to be in the air in five minutes,
to use all my skills
to fly at the speed of sound
to a place I had never been
and had seen only in photographs,
to drop my bomb,
and if I did my job well,

to kill perhaps the parents-to-be
of these very children.

Oh what music the world would have missed.

A Visit to the White House

I was invited to the White House a few summers ago, and I felt right at home there.

But it was not in the way that all Americans should be able to feel at home at the White House; it was in another way. I felt at home with people who hobbled in braces and on crutches, with people on rolling hospital beds, with people who spoke in sign, and with people who in their misshapen bodies struggled to speak and to push the buttons and levers on their self-propelled wheelchairs. And I felt especially at home with children whose behavior was often strange and unpredictable like the behavior of Ronald, my nine-year-old with autism.

We were gathered, these disabled people plus many of us considered by society not to be disabled, for the signing of the Americans with Disabilities Act, July 26, 1990. Not since the passage in the seventies of public law 94-142, the Education of All Handicapped Children Act, has there been a law this significant for disabled people.

And in that mass of two thousand people on the south lawn, every face was glowing with a joy the newly freed slaves must have felt after the Emancipation Proclamation.

After years of suffering the most systematic discrimination in our history, disabled people were about to become free at last.

I have done volunteer work in the disability community for about twenty years, but I was not prepared for the scene at the White House. The minute I entered the southwest gate, I could not contain my tears. All I could do was scribble in my notebook. Some excerpts follow:

There is joy here, a sense of victory, a sense of hope and promise, a sense of empowerment. Empowerment to do what? Only to live, to work, to participate, to prove their worth to society—and to themselves. . . .

Everyone is smiles and cameras. I notice that the hearing-impaired people can use sign to communicate over the noise of the crowd. Those of us dependent on sound can't be heard above the roar. . . .

In the midst of all this, I think of Ronald and his mother, Sally (who at the time of this writing was president of the Autism Society of Iowa), and wish they were here.

The emcee tells everyone to clear the aisles so we can begin. I have news for the emcee: It has already begun. This train is moving, and the officials better just jump on board. . . .

The legislators arrive. Tom Harkin, to great applause. Bob Dole, with his withered hand, moving among the wheelchairs. Orrin Hatch. Bob Michel. Ted Kennedy. Everyone seems to be on the same side of the political aisle today . . .

Former Representative Tony Coehlo shows up. Despite the alleged scandal, the disabled people applaud him vigorously. They know he has epilepsy and they know of his work on this bill. . . .

The President and Mrs. Bush enter to wild cheering and applause. . . .

Looking back at the President, I notice the press corps. They look bored, almost cynical. They are laughing and joking and I think, *of course, this has been staged and it is a "photo op" and there are reasons to doubt the sincerity of some of the politicians—but I'll take it because its importance to these disabled people far transcends the rest of that stuff. . . .*

The Reverend Mr. Harold Wilke, who has no arms, invokes in his prayer the passage, "Let my people go," and prays that the chains of slavery for millions of disabled people will finally be broken. He prays "in the name of God whom we call by many names."

President Bush then rose to speak and said to the crowd, "This day belongs to you." The people went wild again. The President pointed out that the United States is the first country in the world to pass such a law, and he said he was sure many countries would now follow suit.

It was a good speech. He referred to the Berlin Wall, then, as he picked up a pen, he said, "Now as I sign this legislation, we take a sledgehammer to another wall . . . let the shameful wall of exclusion come tumbling down."

When the President rose to leave, he bent over to Evan Kemp of the Equal Employment Opportunity Commission, proud and smiling in a wheelchair, and, it being too awkward to shake Mr. Kemp's hand, kissed him on the forehead.

It was more than some of us grown men could take. I made a final note:

It's 88 degrees. Tears. Sweat. Joy. Triumph. Suddenly, I
see the only empty chair in the whole crowd. I had not
even noticed, yet it is right next to me. And I think of
Ronald and know in my heart that the seat was saved for
him. . . .

The Fellowship of the Wounded

I do not wish misfortune on anyone, but it becomes clearer and clearer that the longer I work within our political and economic system, a law or a new policy suddenly happens when a legislator or executive has a personal connection with the subject at hand.

The most dramatic case in point was the passage of the Americans with Disabilities Act, which had the sponsorship of both Republicans and Democrats, of both the Congress and the Administration, even though there was considerable opposition from the business community.

But Bob Dole is disabled. Tom Harkin, the bill's chief sponsor, has a brother who is deaf. Orrin Hatch had a mentally disabled sibling. Ted Kennedy had a mentally disabled sibling. And so on.

On the day of the passage of the bill, the Senate was alive with emotion, senators in tears, and disabled people in the galleries and lining the hallways. There has probably been no day like it in the history of the Senate.

Just this week I came across a more recent example, this one from the business community. I received a small promotional brochure from B. Dalton describing the bookseller's "Children With Special Needs Collection."

The brochure began with "a message to our readers from Steve Riggio, (who at the time was) Executive Vice President." I quote parts of the message:

My three-year-old daughter, Melissa, has Down syndrome. When she was born, my family and I wanted to gather as much information as we could to help answer our many questions. Yet, I often had difficulty locating useful resources. In time, and with guidance, I found books that addressed my child's needs and, most importantly, showed me how to better realize the joys of raising Melissa. Knowing that such books are available but hard to find led me to start this collection. . . .

I hope that bringing them together in this way has created an invaluable resource for all of you whose lives are touched by children with special needs. . . .

Indeed, the B. Dalton collection *is* a valuable resource, for which I commend Mr. Riggio. But it seems reasonable to wonder if any large bookseller would ever have created such a resource if Mr. Riggio and Melissa had not come along.

My friend Martin Marty, the noted scholar and church historian at the University of Chicago, refers to the "fellowship of the wounded," a way of saying that when we are wounded, in whatever way, we often find our connections through those wounds.

I wish that we found more connection through joy and celebration, but I'm afraid that it is more often through pain that we come together, and more often through pain that we find personal and spiritual growth.

This shared pain is a powerful part of the Alcoholics Anonymous program, and of so many of the programs and groups which have sprung from it. Shared pain is at the center of all the support groups, such as incest survivors and breast-cancer survivors and of the various intentional communities forming around the country.

So I confess that sometimes in my frustration, I find myself thinking, *If only Governor————or Senator———— —or school-board member————or the CEO of———— corporation had a child with a disability, we could get something done.*

It is a selfish and uncharitable thought, and I am ashamed of it, but I do wish that those leaders and decision makers who find themselves (perhaps only temporarily) in the fellowship of the *un*wounded would be more responsive to those of us in the fellowship of the wounded.

Employment Rights and Common Sense

Dear Art:

You know how passionate I am about employment opportunities for people with disabilities, and you have heard me criticize businesspeople for their unwillingness to seize the opportunity to hire these talented and productive people.

But there *is* another side of the coin, one which was brought home to me dramatically at a meeting a few weeks ago.

Two representatives of people with disabilities were giving a presentation about the Americans with Disabilities Act and how it could make a very positive difference to businesses, many of which seem now to see it only as a source of potential litigation.

One of the presenters was the representative of an advocacy group, and the other was a person with a disability, cerebral palsy. As supportive as I am of people with disabilities, I was distressed by what I felt was a very inappropriate use of talent.

As you know, cerebral palsy is a very physically debilitating affliction in which it seems, according to a poem I once read by a person with cerebral palsy, that the mind is imprisoned in a body which will not respond as it should.

People with cerebral palsy have proven over and over

again that they are capable of many jobs, occupations, and professions. And assistive technology is giving them access to even more possibilities for employment.

But usually—and I emphasize *usually*—people with cerebral palsy have great difficulty with speech, and it is often very difficult to understand them. I will never forget my embarrassment and distress when, as president of the Epilepsy Foundation of America presiding at a meeting of people with developmental disabilities, I was unable to understand the question of a young man with cerebral palsy. It was an awful moment for both of us.

I thought of that during the ADA presentation as I tried to understand the comments of the man with cerebral palsy. The program was carefully scripted, with one presenter speaking a while then handing the mike to the other speaker. The audience's inability to, or at least difficulty in, following the continuity of the program undermined both the message and the intended effect.

To make matters worse, the young man stated that his ambition was to be in sales or public relations.

As I sat there, struggling to understand, I could not help but speculate at what might be the reaction of a businessperson who had come to learn and perhaps to consider more open employment for people with disabilities.

Might that businessperson have thought, *Oh, no, what if a person with this problem tries to interview for a sales job or a P.R. job? What then? If I say he is not qualified because he can't be understood, can he sue me?*

A good question, and by now, Art, you know what I'm getting at. It bothers me that we might be facing a gigantic backlash if we who care about employment rights for people with disabilities do not try to impose some discipline and guidelines on ourselves.

It would have been much better for the cause of the ADA, as well as for the general cause of people with disabilities, if the presenters, though disabled, had possessed all the skills necessary to make an effective, persuasive presentation.

Surely, it is not in the interest of the cause for us to support the false belief that a person with a disability is as qualified as anyone else to do *any* job he or she wants to do. And in the case of the young man with cerebral palsy, no one does him a favor by encouraging his clearly unrealistic ambition of being in sales or public relations. In fact, he is being done a drastic disservice by those— teachers, counselors, friends, family—who don't provide an honest evaluation of where his real skills and talents lie.

God knows it is heartrending to hear any young person state an ambition which I know he or she is not qualified to attain—and never will be. But I've had these same feelings about people without disabilities, people judged "normal," who simply lack the aptitude or talent to do a job they passionately want to do.

It is "normal" for employers to try to match talents and abilities with the jobs to be done. And we who advocate for people with disabilities should support that concept and should attempt, in our own efforts, to demonstrate at every opportunity how those talents and abilities can be matched effectively.

Love,
Dad

Who Makes the Decisions
at the Margins of Life?

Dear Clare:

I was very moved by the letter about your visit to the hospital to see your friend and her prematurely born baby, her "preemie," her tiny miracle. It reminded me of a similar situation a few years ago.

Perhaps you remember a photograph that stayed on the refrigerator door for a year or so? It was of a baby hooked up with all kinds of tubes and wires to who knows what kind of machinery; beside the baby was a Coke can which was almost as big as the baby herself.

The photo was a reminder to me of the very miracle of my little friend who is now a healthy, active, mischievous preschooler.

I'm reminded, too, of one of my last visits with my father twelve years ago, just a few months before his death. At the time, Dad was having trouble recognizing people or, at least, coming up with the right names.

Dad, as you know, was never one to spend a lot of time with doctors or hospitals, and was generally suspicious of medical peoples and their wares. So I know he must have resented and been embarrassed by the indignities that hospitals so often visit upon elderly people.

On the particular visit I am remembering, Dad was

sleeping when I arrived. As I watched him, he smiled and moved his body a bit and spoke unintelligible words, still asleep.

I remembered watching dogs sleeping in the shade, barking and running in their sleep. "Those old dogs are happy," Dad had said at the time. "They're dreaming they're chasing a rabbit."

So as I watched him, I thought, *I'll bet he's happy, dreaming that he's preaching a sermon again.*

When I think about the "preemies" of this world who, according to the averages, will face life with some kind of disability, and the elderly people who, it seems to casual observers, have nothing left to live for, I worry that we in this society are moving toward health-care decisions that may cause the people on the margins of life to fall through the cracks.

The ethical issues are daunting, and I do not have the answers, but I worry about how easily ethicality gives way to economics in America.

I worry that, for instance, given a scholarly statistical review of "quality of life" criteria, we can judge some neonatal care not worth the "investment." Where would this leave your friend's baby and my little friend pictured on the refrigerator?

I worry that we can judge an elderly person's life not worth living, and then withhold treatment or technology because the patient's "productive life" is over. I'm sure the definition of "productive life" would not include my father's dreams of preaching a sermon once again. Indeed,

the very nature of the term *productive life* implies usefulness to society.

And once we begin to make judgments about quality of life, about usefulness to society, where does it
stop?

We are not all that many years away from the days of
"warehousing" mentally disabled people to get them out
of the way, then, in some states, sterilizing them. "After
all," experts must have asked themselves in well-meaning
justification, "what kind of quality of life could they have?
How productive could they be?"

I worry that once we allow economic rationales to become the bases of life-and-death decisions, we will begin
to allow terms like *quality of life* and *usefulness* and *productive* to be defined by the technocrats.

In my view, we've suffered enough already from the
tyranny of technocracy. I hope we can keep it out of
moral and ethical health-care decisions.

Having said all this, I admit that there seem to be those
situations in which extraordinary life-saving measures are
fruitless, and In which the definition of life seems highly
technical indeed. That's why I said the ethical issues are
daunting.

It is also why I say let's keep the technocrats in an
advisory and not a decision-making capacity. The decision —the choice—must be personal, preferably in-
volving the patient and the responsible family.

As you know, I have a living will because I don't
want to be kept alive technically and I don't want to

bankrupt my family with the cost of extraordinary life-saving measures. So I leave that choice to no one else.

And I guess there's always some risk involved, but I make that choice and take that risk realizing fully that, even as they are "disconnecting" me, my deep consciousness may be filled with the richest of dreams.

Love,
Dad

THINKING ABOUT SARAH

We know when to celebrate, but
when do we start grieving?
Some say, "As soon as we know
life is ending."
Yet we know that life
is always ending,
and do not grieve every day;
it would be too much
even for a born griever like me.
So years ago we made an agreement with ourselves:
We wait for a doctor to give us the signal,
then we begin to grieve.

But now there's a new question:
What about those tiny lives,
the new ones measured by the ounce
and the minute,
the ones that leave us
not knowing if our tears
are in celebration or in mourning?

With every report from the hospital
I am smiling and grieving,
smiling and grieving.

BARB'S BABY

We come to celebrate Christmas
but hear before the service
that a baby was born
with a collapsed lung and crossed arteries,
near death at birth,
and will require one of the new miracles
if he is to come into life
and walk among us,
if he is ever to light the altar candles
or squirm and giggle through a sermon
or play Joseph in the pageant
or sing in the youth choir,
if he is ever to fall in love
with a blond soprano
and try to sit next to her on the bus
on a spring tour to Washington,
if he is ever to leave home someday
and return only for Christmas,
to sit once again with his parents
and celebrate new life
in the place where now we pray
he will simply survive.

Part Four

Love and Marriage and Parenthood

Zen and the
Art of Diaper Changing

Dear Jim and Rick:

I wonder sometimes how you must feel when you see me with Ronald. Surely you remember, when you were his age, that I was working all the time, gone a lot, frequently arguing with your mother, and always demanding of you.

Now I take Ronald camping and fishing, I spend time helping him learn as much as he can in the ways that he can. I do not demand his perfection, and I am patient in the face of his aggressive behaviors.

This is not intended as a confessional, yet I do confess that I am distressed by how much of me you missed and how much of you I missed. I don't seek forgiveness, yet I do feel impelled to try to gain your understanding. And I will not offer the excuse of time or career demands, yet I did give those excuses at the time.

The real problem was that I had no concept whatsoever of what it really meant to be a parent. I did not know how it was supposed to feel, I did not know what I was supposed to do; I did not understand parenthood as only one side of a truly human relationship in which both parent and child have rights and responsibilities to each other; and I did not understand that parenthood is among the best of life's opportunities for spiritual growth.

I engaged the role of father as "owner." You two were like additions to all the other things your mother and I were acquiring in our young married life. I believe, though I cannot swear to this after so many years, that I thought I was supposed to provide for your health and material welfare and that you were supposed to behave in certain ways that reflected well on your parents, specifically on me.

When you had psychological or emotional problems as a child, Jim, and we took you for therapy, I remember asking the psychologist: "Look, I had *real* problems as the child of a broken home. I can't understand why Jimmy would be having problems."

The psychologist, a wise lady, answered, "Jimmy has impediments you didn't have."

"What impediments?" I asked.

"Parents who are always making sure he understands their expectations."

At the time, that made no sense to me, and I wrote it off as psychological mumbo jumbo.

It took years, until soon after Ronald's birth, for me to undergo what you might call a "conversion experience," and it happened, of all places, at an advertising conference.

There was a morning session for attendees and spouses conducted by Dr. Fernando Bartolome, who at the time was a professor of business administration at Bentley College. Dr. Bartolome had done considerable research with high-level business executives concerning the impact of their business on their personal lives.

The attendees that morning were middle-aged advertising executives, mostly men, and their wives. As the session proceeded, I noticed a palpable change in the room, with some hand-holding and some tears as Dr.

Bartolome described what was missing from the lives of many businesspeople.

Let me back up a minute to remind you that I could never change dirty diapers when you were infants. I could not stand the smell; I gagged and had to leave the room. I figured that I just had some allergy to bad smells. At the time of this advertising conference, I was using these same excuses during Ronald's infancy.

Now back to Dr. Bartolome. At one point toward the end of the session he asked, "How many of you remember being sick at your stomach, rushing into the bathroom, and vomiting?"

Most people raised their hands.

"How many of you remember your mothers coming in with a cool washcloth, putting it on your forehead, and touching you as you vomited, comforting you?"

Most people raised their hands.

"How many of you remember your fathers doing that?"

There were no hands. None. Not one.

Dr. Bartolome paused a long time then said, "Just think." He paused again for emphasis. "Just think what your fathers missed that they will never have the chance to experience because they were never in that moment with you in your need. Just think of the opportunities for growth and bonding that they missed, gone forever."

His unspoken point, of course, was that we middle-aged men in that room had most likely missed that same opportunity.

But not me, I thought, and when I returned home I

said to Sally, "Okay, let me at those diapers. I'm not going to miss that experience any longer."

And I didn't. I remember so well trying to hold my breath (and my tongue in my cheek) while smiling at Ronald and saying things like, "No matter how wretched this diaper is, Ron, I am in this moment, and I just know I'm growing from this experience."

You know something? I *was* growing, just as I am growing from writing this letter to you today. Which brings me to my purpose in writing. I simply wanted to say this:

While I regret my shortcomings as a young father to you, I understand also that regret in itself is a fairly worthless emotion unless it produces a positive reaction. In my case, part of that positive reaction is manifest in my parenting of Ronald, which I hope you will interpret not only within the context of my relationship with him, but also as a demonstration of what I would do with both of you if I could travel in time. I feel deeply that the experience of being Ronald's father has also enriched my experience of being your father.

And this: I understand that being a parent never ends and that it has the opportunity for growth and the power to continually transform us right up to the last breath.

With gratitude and love,
Dad

The Hard Truth About Talent

Dear Jim:

One of the most difficult and perplexing things to deal with in the world is this: Talent does not guarantee success.

If it did, there would not be so many *good* musicians playing on street corners. Or there would not be so many *good* writers who have to do something else for a living.

You've heard that old cliché: I have to work as a hobby to support what I'm really supposed to do in the world.

And of course, in saying talent doesn't guarantee success, we're talking about success by the world's definition which you and I could boil down to simply making enough income from our callings or our chosen field that we can work and live and grow without having to do something else.

There was a recent popular book entitled something like, "Do What You Love, the Money Will Follow." I guess I can agree with that to the extent that it didn't say *how much* money would follow.

But if we agree not to debate about the definition of success or how much income is enough for working and living and growing within your chosen field, then we come right back to the originial proposition: Talent does not guarantee success.

What does it guarantee then?

Answer: nothing.

It doesn't even guarantee your own satisfaction, your own fulfillment. How many of your fellow musicians are very talented yet frustrated, disappointed, disillusioned, and even angry? And haven't you, as talented as you are, felt the same way?

No, talent guarantees nothing.

It is only how we feel about that talent, how we set ourselves to build on it and grow with it, and what we set ourselves to do with it that gives the satisfaction and fulfillment and happiness.

You and I remember a wonderful neighbor who was a very talented banjo player and folk singer. He had sung with a group, and I suspect there was a time when he thought he would take his talent into show business and become a performer full-time. But he did not. He went into another profession, got married, had children.

And what is our memory of him? Sitting on the back porch, gathering the neighborhood children around, and playing and singing with them. I know he grew from that simple experience of sharing his talent and I know he felt rewarded, though he made his living at something else.

This reality is not restricted to the creative arts. There are firms full of lawyers who are more talented than the senior partners; companies with middle managers who can motivate people to results that the CEO could never have achieved; universities with untenured faculty whose talents as scholars and teachers could put some tenured professors in the shade; churches with ministers whose talents for making God's love manifest in the everyday world far surpass those of their perhaps more administratively astute seniors. I could go on.

The point is that what talent provides is the instrument of your own growth and fulfillment through how you choose to use it. I know this is difficult to grasp and take comfort in as you struggle to make a go of the band. But as you are learning on every road trip you take, the real joy comes in playing, in making something work in community with the other band members, in seeing the happiness and response of the audience, the people who appreciate and enjoy and are moved by your talents.

Embrace and hold on to those joyful experiences, Jim, for they are the only true rewards of talent.

Love,
Dad

Keep Your Eyes on
the Things You Cannot See

Dear Art:

When I was in jet fighter training and on my first night flight over the west Texas oil fields, my instructor told me to close my eyes. I felt him maneuver the plane but did not know what he'd done. It felt like an aileron roll.

"Open your eyes," he said, "and take the stick."

I did. Everything looked normal. Stars and constellations above, oil well and ranch house lights below.

What had he done, I wondered, other than roll?

Then the plane began to act weird. The nose wanted to go up. I pushed the stick forward, throwing both my instructor and me against our seat belts and shoulder harnesses.

"What the hell?" I muttered.

I was completely confused, and felt almost out of control before I realized, over my instructor's laughter through the intercom, that those "stars and constellations" were oil well and ranch house lights—and vice versa.

My instructor had simply rolled the plane exactly inverted, then given me control.

"Strange," I said, rolling out and recovering from the dive.

"You see what you expect to see," my instructor said. "Don't ever trust that."

I'm writing this in response to your frustration and anger with your boss who, after all the work you did on an analysis, made a decision that seemed to ignore the facts. You may be right; perhaps she made the wrong decision. I have no way of knowing, so all I can offer as advice is, please be open to the possibility that she may be seeing something you're not.

It's funny how clearly I now see the symbolic and metaphorical value of earlier experiences like my first night flight, as well as experiences in business. But at the time, they were just experiences which I took absolutely at face value.

Perhaps my old jet instructor was the first person to tell me not to always believe my eyes, then many years later, another man I respected, my mentor in business, told me, "It is important to keep your eyes on the things you cannot see."

If at this point, you're wondering how to do that—in business or in life—I turn to a quote from another pilot, Antoine de Saint-Exupéry: "It is only with the heart that one can see rightly. What is essential is invisible to the eye."

I guess this letter boils down to some pretty old, basic, and, some would say, romantic stuff: Do what your heart *shows* you to do.

Love,
Dad

A Father's Pride and Joy

(August 1991)

Dear Friends:

These days I am filled with a sense of joy and celebration about Ronald who, as most of you know, has autism.

He has just completed his first year as a fully integrated kindergartner in a Des Moines public school. There was a little resistance at first to his full integration, but the school principal and teacher agreed to give it a try. His schedule was tough—half days in the autism class and half days in kindergarten.

There were two other children with autism assigned to his class, and a teacher's aide was assigned to help the three "special" students.

Ronald quickly became a full-fledged member of the class and participated in everything.

Sally and I noticed real changes in Ronald, and as he learned the alphabet and some reading and some number skills, we became elated.

Then this spring he was given the "first grade entrance exam." That's my term for it; it was actually a readiness test. The teacher adapted the test so that he did not have to circle answers or do other fine-motor-skill things, but could just say the answer or point to it. Result: he got forty-six of forty-eight answers correct. In other words, they tested what he knew, *not* how well he took the test.

Sally and I were simply overjoyed, and I've been bragging for the past month.

We know Ronald still will have problems, with learning, with behavior, with social skills. We don't ever kid ourselves. But the future does look brighter.

Still, there is something about having a child with a disability, something always present, something inescapable. On the one hand is the blessing and joy of Ronald; on the other is the fear.

I wrote the following poem while on vacation, as I realized that the fears about Ronald are never far below the surface. It says more than I could ever write in prose or ever explain to anyone about how it feels sometimes.

VACATION POEM

How the thing with Ronald
pushes through, as soon as we relax,
away on a vacation,
alone, quiet.
It comes without form
but a presence nonetheless.
Heavy. Intruding. Calling
us away from our pleasure
as if pleasure is no longer allowed,
as if we must always be aware,
constantly dealing with
this thing,
this fear,
this future.

I can't read this poem without crying, yet I know I cry for myself, not for Ronald.

What I realize is that I must stay focused on what I have to do to help his future, and that I can do something every single day to make his future better. Also, to help fend off the "thing," the demon in that poem, I know I must stay focused on what he is doing today and how he is doing today.

And how is he doing? Well, friends, as of today, he's one of the top graduates in his kindergarten class. A blessing. A treasure. A father's pride and joy.

With love to you all,
Jim

P.S. Editor's note: Ronald is now ten and fully integrated into third grade.

ORDINARY CHILDREN

I get tired of seeing competent children,
with facile fingers writing,
tying shoes, buttoning shirts, zipping jackets,
playing complicated games
on computers,
or throwing balls at bats
and in baskets.
I get tired of those agile little bodies
on bicycles or skateboards
shifting their weight and balancing,
jumping curbs or dodging one another,
the way competent children do ordinary things.
They are the daily reminders,
these ordinary children of other parents,
and I get tired of being reminded.

FELLOW TRAVELERS

A boy stutters to me,
his eyes askew behind thick glasses,
about airplanes and coming home from Florida,
about the weather and cars
and anything else that crosses his mind
in these few minutes,
and I recognize him instantaneously,
and want to rush to his parents
and take their hands and,
through the distress and fatigue
they feel changing planes at O'Hare
with this strange and unpredictable child,
cry Yes Yes I know I know
and Don't despair
and We're all in this together
and Despite everything,
it's worth it.

A Letter for the Future

Dear Ronald:

Even though you will not be able to read and understand this letter for a few years, this is my way of pledging to you that you *will* have a place in business and that business will be better because of your place in it.

My heart breaks sometimes because of what you are still to go through, things you do not now expect and would not understand—just as now you do not understand that many of your third-grade friends accommodate your strange behaviors and still think of you as their friend. To them you are, simply, "Ronald," with all your academic difficulties and your sometimes goofy compulsions.

You cannot know how this will change, but it will. Within a few years, as these other children begin to form their cliques, you will not be included. (Your first taste of that came just last week when the other kids would not let you play soccer.)

As a teenager, you will likely suffer, as do so many other teenagers with autism, by not knowing the appropriate things to say or the appropriate ways to behave and, at the same time, by knowing that you do not know those things. In other words, the normal awkwardness of teenagers will be magnified many times in your life.

These experiences are inevitable unless there is some major medical breakthrough in basic biomedical brain research—and there is not likely to be such a breakthrough within the decade.

It is also inevitable that, with the help of friends and family, you will get through those years. If you continue to learn as you have been learning, there is a good chance you will go to college. Then you will graduate and go to work. And business will be ready for you.

You see, Ronald, there are things you do, talents you have which can help you throughout your life. Memory is one. Though you focus it now on memorizing such prodigious challenges as all the dialogue and lyrics to *The Music Man,* you will learn to harness it as part of your work. Concentration is another. When you decide to concentrate on something, such as tossing rocks in a bucket—as aimless as that seems now—it tells me that you will be able to concentrate on your job, whatever that may be.

By the time you read this, you may not remember a man your mom and I introduced you to several months ago. His name is Bill, and he has autism.

As of this writing, Bill works at a major Fortune 500 corporation. He is in a beginning position, but I know he will work his way up as long as he sticks to those things he does better than anyone else. You see, he too has a wonderful memory and he too has the ability to focus his attention on doing something the same way, time after time.

Bill is of an earlier era in the history of the treatment of autism. If he has done as well as he has, then I am encouraged that you will be able to do even better.

And by the time you come into the workplace, a lot of the battles of prejudice and discrimination will have been won, thanks, in large part, to people like Bill. And to people like Bill's supervisor, a wonderful woman, a true corporate hero, who had to convince her boss and her boss's boss that Bill was the person for the job.

Bill's success vindicates the courage and good judgment of his supervisor; his personality and his very person speak for all people with disabilities. He brightens the offices and is admired and appreciated for who he is as well as for what he does. He is, in a way, a present-day pioneer.

I confess to you, my beautiful son, that I have cried myself to sleep many times since your mom and I first found out something was "wrong." She and I have mourned the death of the child who never was, but I assure you also that 99 percent of the time, we celebrate the child who is: *you*.

In fact, I would not change who you are or what you have been through or what we have gone through together. However, I would like to change the future you face, and the best way for me to do that is to be present with you every day, teaching, supporting, comforting, and yes, positively disciplining you toward a life of self-esteem, independence, and contribution to society.

And believe me, you will have much to contribute.

Love,
Dad

Do As I Say and Not as I Did

Dear Art:

I am more than willing to give you some man-to-man observations about marriage, but Lord knows I am not exactly the person *I* would choose for advice about marriage. Yes, as you said, Sally and I seem to have gotten it "right," but it is her second marriage and my third—not exactly the record you would want to emulate.

On the other hand, what we have learned the hard way about marriage might have some value for you—not that marriages can be easily generalized, and not that you won't have to do your own learning when all is said and done.

The world is full of good people and their writings about the kind of commitments and the kind of understandings required to be fulfilled in a marriage. I would not attempt that kind of advice.

But let me just share a thought on one subject so vital to young working people these days—the balance in work life and personal life:

It slips up on you.

It seduces you.

Both of you are working and productive and happy. Both of you come home and talk about the day and your accomplishments. You have friends in the same circumstance, so when you get together for an evening, all of you talk about your days and your accomplishments.

The next thing you know, you have slipped into a kind of professional marriage, a relationship in which the admixtures of work life and family life seem so natural and desirable and become so intertwined and mutually dependent that you lose balance. Then, when only one element changes—a promotion missed, a child lagging in school, a serious illness, or a layoff by the company—the marriage comes crashing down around your shoulders.

You know I believe that work is part of life and that the two should not be treated dualistically—that is, you should not try to be one person at work and a different person at home—but I also believe that either personal life or work life can become so compulsively preoccupying that it begins to destroy the other.

Usually for men, I'm afraid, the work life is the culprit. Why? Because we usually work harder at making our work lives fulfilling than we do at making our home and family lives fulfilling. I'm sure some man somewhere has let home and family life destroy the work life, but in thirty-three years in business, I've never seen it.

On the other hand, I believe that women, sometimes by choice but more often because they have no choice, face the opposite situation. They find themselves in family circumstances that preclude them from some professional opportunities. I also observe with admiration that women seem much less inclined to turn their family lives upside down for the sake of career.

Where is the middle ground? I'm not sure exactly, because when I was starting out, as you are, I did not find it. But I believe the balance begins with a commitment about several fairly straightforward yet complex things: love, marriage, family, community, career, money, and life-style.

Ask yourself this question: Would I sacrifice my career for the sake of my marriage and family? Please note that the question is *not,* Would I want to, or like to, sacrifice my career for the sake of my marriage and family? But, simply, Would I? No ifs, ands, or buts. No conditions. No negotiating. Just yes or no.

If the answer is no, then ask for the ring back, tell S— to stop working on the dress, and cancel the church date. Of course, the chances are you won't ever have to sacrifice your career for your marriage or family, but if you're not honestly willing to do it, your marriage is already in jeopardy.

If the answer is yes, you're on the right track. But short of sacrificing your love and marriage, both of you also need to commit to supporting each other's careers, because work itself has spiritual value, and the growth possible from what you have set yourselves to do as a vocation can make you richer people, which then can enrich your marriage and your lives together.

But be aware of this also: Despite the talk about family values these days, society generally supports work life to a much greater degree than it supports family life. So recognize this and try to find a company or a career that supports family life; at the very least, avoid a company that rewards you for neglecting your family life.

After your family and your work, comes a commitment to your community, to sharing your cumulative richness with your friends, your extended family, the members of your church and other organizations, and with those less fortunate.

If you then can live these commitments, everything else

will follow. Parenthood, that greatest of human blessings, will feel right and good from the beginning, though that will change your lives more than you can ever imagine.

And chances are, your life-style will reflect your balance by not becoming overly focused on money or the things money buys. Money is right up there next to sex in its power to disrupt your lives.

I wish I could boil all this down to an easy-to-follow set of guidelines, which you surely can find in some volume of homespun philosophy somewhere, but I can't. I believe it is largely a matter of establishing your own principles early on, then making the rest of it fit your principles and not the other way around.

Of course, I could offer this little guideline: Do as I say and not as I did.

Love,
Dad

CORPORATE MARRIAGE

She was more like his oldest daughter
though I doubt even a daughter
would have taken those scoldings
or settled for an allowance
or accepted a last will and testament
that guaranteed his immortality
by controlling the money from the grave,
as if assigning his financial ghost
to make sure that she in her girlish ways
would not squander the hard-earned estate.

He thought she had it made,
a good life,
more than her parents ever expected her to have
and all she had to do was marry him,
give him children,
entertain his guests,
and look the right part
in the right place
at the right time.
*Not such a bad assignment
in the scheme of things,* he thought.

When she moved out her explanation was,
as he would have expected, foolish:
"I'm the one with the master's degree after all."
It was not rational enough
for him to take apart,

listing and examining each element
in his reliable decision-tree method,
so he finally concluded that
"If a problem is not rational
what am I supposed to do about it?"

This is an old story,
a cliché even,
about the failed marriage of a corporate exec.
You've heard it all before
and you know what comes next,
the shock of friends
and puzzlement of the grown children,
attempts to keep it out of the papers,
a settlement that would be
referred to ever after as generous,
and plays and replays at the clubs
and on the golf courses,
those conversations ending always with the hope
that perhaps with a little luck
time will take care of it,
and people can get back to business.

A WEDDING POEM AT 30,000 FEET

For Doug Green and Marion Jambor-Green

Thinking about you
and how your lives have blossomed and faded
and blossomed again
with moments of love lost and found
on the way finally
to one single day in October,
I wonder what words can possibly celebrate
such a journey.
I have no vocabulary,
I give up.
There are plenty of poems
and I will choose someone else's,
a fine poem, a classic perhaps.

Then, floating in the light turbulence of a clear sky
(a sign that there can be turbulence
even in the clearest conditions),
I look over at Sally
dozing with that serenity she carries
from day into night,
from waking into sleeping and back again,
a calm I can only imagine
but which I know bears me through each day.
And I am moved one more time to find the words,
to bring up from somewhere a sense,
even a hint,
of what it is to understand at last

how the love of one person can deliver us
into a life we didn't even know we believed in.
Not a life without pain or anger or hurt or disappointment;
to the contrary, a life with all of that,
and yet,
a life without despair.

Is this all I can write for you, Doug and Marion,
on this happy day,
not a poem of blessing
for a love of excitement and pleasure and comfort,
but instead for a love that promises only
that you are delivered forever from despair?
Yes, my friends, yes.
I can do no more,
for this is love's only guarantee.

Part Five

Businessman at Random

Living in the Nowness

I've written many times about how important it is for a manager to truly listen—"active listening" they call it in the workshops.

I discovered during my years in management that in order to listen, I needed to be present. Sounds ridiculous on the surface, doesn't it? *Of course,* in order to listen, one needs to be present.

But I don't mean being present, as in simply being in the same room at the same time, I mean *present,* as in clearheaded, focused, and paying full attention to the speaker.

There's the old business expression in describing a meeting: "It was a MEGO meeting." Translation: "My Eyes Glazed Over." It's what we say when we can just no longer pay attention. If it happens, as it did plenty of times in those endless strategic planning meetings or budget review meetings, no real harm is done.

But when it happens in a one-on-one meeting with an employee, there is serious, perhaps irreparable, harm done. Anyone can tell when a listener is tuned in or tuned out, and no manager I know has mastered the trick of smiling and nodding convincingly while thinking about something else. If you think you have, you're kidding yourself and need to wake up. After all, you can't expect an employee to risk confronting you with your inattention.

Yet, I've committed the sin of inattention, and I'm sure you will also. It's a temptation when you're hearing the same complaint or the same pitch for the umpteenth time. You're sure you know what is being said and what is going to be said. There'll be nothing new, no surprises, no insights, nothing at all to compensate you for the time you're "giving."

It is important, though, to realize that the value of listening is in the listening itself and what it communicates to the other person: involvement and, often, empathy. There is a value to you as well, though sometimes it's tough to feel it, and that is in being *connected* through your willingness to truly be present with this person at this time and in this place.

The cultivation of that "presence" is as important as any other skill you'll learn in your careers.

I learned it over a long period of time, but the most significant influence on my own ability to be present was my conversations with, and observations of, people who consistently practiced some kind of discipline of the inner life, such as meditation, the martial arts, regular prayer, one of the fine arts, or sometimes a physical activity such as jogging done meditatively.

Part of what they taught me is the Eastern philosophy that life takes place in the present, in the now, in the "nowness," as the Buddhists say. I frequently was told: "If you're angry, you're living in the past, and if you're fearful, you're living in the future. To live in the now, you must be neither angry nor fearful."

Larry Wilson, of the Pecos River Learning Center, likes to tell the story of the Zen monk who was walking along one day, minding his business as Zen monks do, when a tiger began to chase him.

The monk ran to a cliff, grabbed a vine hanging there, and let himself over the precipice, thus escaping the tiger. As he was making his way, he looked down to see another tiger at the bottom of the cliff.

Dangling there, trapped between the tigers, he looked up a few feet to see a mouse crawl out of a crevice and begin chewing on the vine.

Then, looking to his left a few feet, he saw a wild strawberry vine with one red ripe luscious strawberry. Holding on with one hand, the monk reached over and picked the strawberry. Then he ate it.

And he enjoyed it!

That's what I call living in the nowness.

We are always dangling between the tiger of the past and the tiger of the future. Those tigers may be serious or they may be as inconsequential as a meeting or business trip. Whatever they are, they are not as important to this moment, to now, as what you are doing at this moment, now.

So here's a little exercise I have found useful for several years. When you feel yourself drifting away, when you need to be present, take a deep breath, think of that Zen monk, exhale, and say to yourself, *Nowness.*

Ever Hear of
Assistive Technology?

Okay, take off your glasses, those of you wearing them. When you do, will you be able to read this page? Or a more pointed question is, without those glasses, would you be able to do your job?

If you answer *no,* then it's fair to say you have a disability that prevents you from earning a livelihood in the way you do now. The thing that overcomes your disability, thus returning you to "normal," is called, by those of us who work in the disability-rights field, "assistive technology."

Hearing aids are in the same category. So are pacemakers. So are wheelchairs. So are synthesized voice devices. So are many other things. For that matter, most "normal" people could not do their jobs these days without some kind of assistive technology, from pencils to word processors. (An earlier name for assistive technology is, simply, *tool.*)

As you can see, once we accept that most of us have a disability of one sort or another and that most of those disabilities can be made irrelevant by assistive technology, then we can stop focusing our attention on the disabilities of people and focus instead on the results the people are able to achieve.

A Definition of Heaven and Hell

I don't know where I heard this, but I pass it along in the hope that it will make you think again about the old concept of reciprocity; that is, the more love (or power or trust) you give others, the more you will receive.

Here's the definition: "Hell is a place where all the people have their elbows broken so they will not be able to feed themselves. Heaven is a place where all the people have their elbows broken so they can more easily feed one another."

Observations of a Speaker

As you know, I frequently speak and lead workshops for companies, communities, and various organizations, both for-profit and nonprofit.

Usually near the beginning of a talk, I read a poem from *Love and Profit.* When I look up from that reading and try to get a feel of the audience, I invariably notice that the women are focused and attentive and are sitting in an "open" position, arms unfolded and body leaning forward, faces relaxed and often smiling. The men are sitting with arms and legs crossed tightly and often are looking at their feet, brow furrowed and face frowning.

Those are generalizations, of course, but they describe the majority reaction from each gender.

At this point, I know things are about normal. The way I know I am finally getting belief and response from the men is when those arms and legs begin to uncross and when their faces begin to lose that worried look.

I've often wondered what they were worried about. How much damage can one little poem do?

A Thought About Injustice

I take very seriously the role of business and its impact on society. I shudder when I hear some businessperson say, "It's just business," because that usually means something is being done in the name of business that would not be done if that person were doing it in the name of himself or herself.

Always remember this: If we can commit an injustice in the name of business, we can commit an injustice in the name of anything.

I Love Schwarzkopf

Forget the celebrity and the sixty-thousand-dollar speaking fees. If anyone deserved to have the star system work for him, it is General Norman Schwarzkopf.

I loved it when he told Barbara Walters that he did not trust a man who couldn't cry.

I loved it when, at his retirement, he told his troops, "I shall always love you and will never, ever, ever forget you." He said this, of course, while wiping tears from his eyes.

I admire him for his military heroism, to be sure, but I also admire him for his courage in showing us his emotional commitment to his calling and to his people.

Okay, I confess that I'm being a little self-serving. After having been told so many times that my demand for emotional honesty in business is "too soft," I find I can now say, "Tell it to Stormin' Norman."

Magic Tricks for the Customers

I observed a real lesson about business and relationships recently on a TWA DC-9 between St. Louis and Des Moines. There was the usual complement of flight attendants, but for some reason, this group was particularly upbeat, smiling, bantering with the passengers, helping several elderly passengers get settled and become comfortable.

About halfway through the short flight, one of the flight attendants, a handsome young man named Stephen, began to do some magic tricks, to the delight of the passengers. He was a good amateur magician and obviously enjoyed sharing his talent. Before we knew it, we were landing.

I am a veteran traveler and generally have the attitude that if the plane gets up and gets down and I'm able to walk away from it, the flight is successful. But even I felt more upbeat and definitely more positive about TWA as a result of this fifty-minute encounter with those flight attendants.

The lesson for business starts with a question: What are the most important jobs on an airliner? Simple: aircrew—pilot, copilot (or first officer) and on some planes, second officer—the people who are responsible for operating the airplane and getting it to the destination safely and without incident.

But safety is no longer a criterion for selecting an airline, at least for the great majority of passengers. Safety is simply *expected*.

The criteria are, as in so many businesses, price and service.

Since airfares, except during certain short-term periods, generally are the same, I contend that the customer service—from ticket agents, baggage handlers, and most especially the cabin crew—becomes increasingly the determining factor for people's choice of an airline, given comparable departure and arrival schedules.

It is as if the customer is saying, Of course, you get me there safely. As for the widely vaunted "on-time" performance, no airline can second-guess the weather or air-traffic delays or mechanical problems. What the customer wants to know is, How are you going to *treat* me?

For other businesses, "safety" equates with "quality." It is simply not good enough to brag about product quality. Quality, like safety for the airlines, is now *expected*. Of course, a product should be trouble-free; of course, it should be dependable; of course, it should be durable.

The question is, again, How are you going to *treat* me?

It should not take a magician to understand that these days, business is all about relationships.

Of course, a little magic couldn't hurt.

Aristocrats at Heart

There need not be another word written about Americans' fascination with the British royal family, but it takes no particular brilliance to observe that Americans seem also driven to create their own royalty of sorts.

The president and his family are obvious examples. I believe people were far more fascinated with Reagan than with Carter. Jimmy Carter carried his own bags and tried to bring a populist simplicity to the White House. It did not sit well with the people. It was as if the average folks were saying, "If *I* were president, *I* wouldn't carry my own bags." It didn't seem right somehow.

Reagan, on the other hand, became like royalty, the benevolent and beloved ruler of the land.

Although this country was founded by people who rejected royalty and aristocracy, I believe that in our hearts, we want to be aristocrats.

Corporations constantly play into these desires. In fact, the perks showered on top executives of corporations provide a life of comfort and convenience probably comparable to that of some of the old European aristocracy. Although I think a lot of the perks are unnecessary, overdone, and frequently of negative impact among the employees, I confess I personally got a kick out of riding on Learjets and in limousines, of rubbing elbows with people whose positions made them "celebrities." It's pretty intoxicating stuff.

Also, as managers move through the middle toward the top, there is a surprising acceptance of the perks, even though not 1 percent of those managers will make it into the senior executive ranks.

And any knowledgeable legislator will tell you that it is not only the wealthy people who resist making inheritance taxes more restrictive; it is average people whose estates will probably never even exceed the family exemption level.

Some say this fascination with aristocracy and this tolerance for extremely disproportionate income and wealth distribution is borne of ignorance or a distorted sense of reality.

That could be true, but I believe also that it is tied very directly to what we call The American Dream. People still believe it is possible for them to "make it," and when they do, damned if they don't plan to "live like a king and then leave what's left to the kids."

What's Your Definition of Moonlighting?

At no time during my thirty years of management did I prohibit employees from free-lancing for other companies, as long as those companies were not directly competitive and as long as the employees did the work on their own time.

That seems a reasonable policy to me. I believe the companies that prohibit free-lancing or moonlighting are assuming that because they are buying the time and skills of an employee for an agreed-upon number of hours per week or month, they deserve to have control over *all* the employee's time.

I am provoked to this subject after reading the profile of a chief executive officer who stated flatly that his employees were not allowed to free-lance or moonlight for other companies. "We feel we pay them enough," he said, "that they can use their nonworking time for family time and personal renewal."

I endorse his feeling that people should focus on family time and personal renewal, but frankly, whether his employees choose to use their personal time that way is none of his business.

The same article pointed out how many corporate boards this same CEO serves on.

I may be simpleminded about this, but will somebody please tell me the difference between an employee moonlighting on his or her own time, within the ethical considerations of such things, and the CEO serving as a *paid* member of another company's board of directors (usually, I might add, *without* taking vacation time to do it and, in some cases, using the company plane to get there)?

I've heard all those explanations about how board service "broadens a CEO" and gives "insights" and builds "contacts" and all that.

I accept the explanations, but they don't negate the fact of the double standard, and they don't negate the fact that often these free-lance board memberships are also just a show of status and privilege.

Schmoozing with the Enemy

When serving on the program committee for the conference of some industry or another, I always joked that the committee's true challenge was not in finding speakers and workshop leaders, but in fitting the "program" in between breakfast and the first tee time, and in being sure the banquet speaker will be brief so that people won't leave before the sports awards are announced.

I think it is this concentration on schmoozing and on leisure in beautiful resort areas that makes so many people, including congresspeople and the IRS, so suspicious about industry conferences, sales meetings, and other such business gatherings which some call boondoggles.

I have been as critical as anyone of wasteful business expenses which ultimately drive up the prices of products, but you know something? In my opinion, those meetings are important to the doing of business, and the schmooze time may be the most important part of them.

The industry conferences are often a too-rare opportunity for competitors to get together. As you know, the laws are very strict about what competitors are allowed to discuss. They are not, for instance, to discuss pricing which could lead to price-fixing.

But there are other "official" subjects important to discuss, such as specification standards for certain kinds of products, training standards and qualifications for certain jobs; initiatives in education; public-service efforts (the Advertising Council comes to mind); initiatives in legislation and regulation; and so on.

But it is the "unofficial" part of the agenda that grows in importance as the business environment grows more competitive. We are so given to turning our business competitiveness into a substitute for war and for turning healthy personal desires to succeed into attitudes of hostility that we need a forum, a setting, in which we can get to know, and enjoy being with, our "enemies."

Then as the years go by in the increasingly changing business world, with people and jobs moving constantly, we become more careful about whom we call the enemy—one, because chances are, we've gotten to know that person, and two, because we may just end up working for him or her someday.

In other words, I have found those conferences not to be boondoggles, but rather civilizing influences. And Lord knows we could use more civilizing influences these days.

The Paradoxes

A young manager friend asked me to "list the paradoxes of management" sometime. I've usually avoided doing it because I don't think I know all the paradoxes of management and because I think some of them are not just restricted to management. But fools rush in, so here I go:

The leader must

- be long-term and short-term at the same time, assuring that the quarterly earnings of the company meet the financial requirements set by the board while often sacrificing short-term earnings in order to assure the long-term growth and development of the company and its stakeholders
- be in touch and aware of what's going on without looking over people's shoulders
- inspire and often direct people in accomplishing the vision and mission and purpose of the organization while empowering people to manage themselves and make their own decisions
- accept and perform the role of spokesperson for the company, the person in the spotlight, the person upon whom much attention is showered while letting go of ego and control and becoming a resource for the employees
- encourage and support the rights and the growth and the independent thinking of individual employees without sacrificing the rights and growth

and interdependence of the community of employees
- care for people and fire people, sometimes the same people
- encourage risk-taking and reward mistakes while preventing any mistakes that could jeopardize the survival of the enterprise
- embrace with full commitment the demands and responsibilities, as well as the rewards, of the job with all its paradoxes while embracing with full commitment the demands and responsibilities, as well as the rewards, of being a parent and spouse and friend

Surprise Me!

We've all known, and probably worked for, a manager who claimed to trust his people to do their jobs and produce results, while at the same time saying such things as, "I don't like surprises. Never under any circumstances surprise me."

It was another way of saying, "I'm in charge, and part of being in charge is knowing *everything* that's going on around here."

Find a manager today who demands no surprises, and I'll show you a manager not ready to take on the challenges of the nineties, because he or she is still stuck in the past with the old command/control ways of doing things. I'll also show you a manager not likely to survive in management for very much longer.

As organizations flatten, it is imperative that managers let go of the illusion of control and realize that their only reasonable course is to preach the vision over and over again; to assure that jobs and performance standards are clearly understood and that behaviors are aligned with values; to set high standards; to hold high expectations; then to trust the people to achieve the results, while at the same time being a resource and support for their efforts.

If the manager's slogan is "No Surprises," it might as well be "No Growth." Inherent in this way of doing things is the understanding that the manager will *never again* know everything that's going on all the time. Furthermore, if the manager does know everything that's going on, it should be a danger signal that there's not enough innovation, not enough individual initiative, perhaps not enough empowerment throughout the organization.

Indeed, the manager's new slogan for the nineties and into the next century had better be, "Surprise me!"

Bread upon the Waters

Of all the expressions of congratulations and support I received last year when I decided to change careers after thirty-two years, the most moving were the notes and letters I received from employees and former employees.

Frequently, they cited something such as a note or letter I had written to them, perhaps years before, expressing sympathy or congratulations. I know that, at the time, those little acts of caring had been part of my everyday activities, sandwiched in among a jillion other things.

Yet, as I read these outpourings of remembrance and affection and support, I began to understand the full meaning of "bread upon the waters" and how it returns to us manyfold.

Our One Shared Value?

Recently, when a conversation among friends turned to the usual indictment of America's materialism, I found myself once again saying that materialism has taken a bum rap.

Of course, there are shelves and shelves of worthless junk out there in consumerland, but there are also all kinds of products that enhance lives, that give us more time together, that take people—particularly stay-at-home parents and spouses—away from some of the drudgery of earlier times, no matter how we may romanticize those times.

"Listen," I say, "I helped build fires for big black washpots down by the creek, and carried buckets of water to boil. As a child, I watched the women of my family deal with those hand-scalding chores one day every week while also doing everything else to be done that day."

And I tell of the dangers of toddlers around the fires and the hot water. I don't remember any serious accidents in my family, but we lived with the stories of washday tragedies in other families.

The next day, of course, the women heated irons on the woodstove for ironing, another finger-burning, back-breaking job.

We may gaze dreamily at the paintings of those joyful washdays by the creek, and we may decorate our early-American family rooms with washpots of flowers and old irons by the fireplace, but the greatest liberator of my mother and her relatives was an old roller washing machine.

"Well, of course," my friends said, "there have been important advances in products, but look at all the unnecessary stuff now. What possible good does it do?"

Then my English professor/poet friend Melvin Wilk spoke up. "A lot of the products themselves may not be all that valuable in people's lives," he said, "but we can say that we do have one fully shared value in this country, the value of buying things as a source of happiness and joyful activity."

The friends were stunned by Mel's obviously serious theory.

He continued, "Just go to a mall and tell me how many unhappy-looking people you see. Most of the people I see there—not all, of course—are smiling. And this value of shopping as a source of joyful activity transcends right and left and knows no particular political philosophy. For that matter, it also transcends racial, gender, religious, and ethnic issues. Everyone does it and everyone does it together."

The more I've thought about Mel's comments, the more I've come to believe he's absolutely right. And his idea is compatible with the contention of some social commentators that malls are the new village greens where people come to promenade, where friends meet, where young men and women do part of their romantic dance.

It makes sense to me, and it's an idea that retailers should pay more attention to.

You're Gonna Get Sued

In the last three years or so of my career as a senior corporate executive, I spent about as much time with lawyers as I did with some of my managers. Our company was a rather benign place in that, in the grand scheme of things, we were not in businesses with a high legal risk.

But we were sued. Some we settled as nuisances. Some we lost. Some we won. Most dragged out a long time and took more time and attention than they deserved.

Still, I think businesspeople spend too much time worrying about getting sued, and they fail to do some important things out of fear of being sued.

Listen. When the decisions are in the manager's hands, the manager should do what he or she thinks is right, and to hell with worrying about lawsuits. Seek legal advice, sure. Assess risks, sure. Then do the right thing.

And understand this: You are going to be sued. One of the good things about America is that we have the right to litigate. You can't keep people from suing you, some of them unfairly and frivolously. And you can't keep from becoming upset from time to time by unfair claims, but you also can't let the fear of lawsuits paralyze you.

Celebrities and Unsung Heroes

If you've read this far, you know I am an ex-jet fighter pilot. I'm also an inveterate airshow watcher. Last year, I went to see the U.S. Air Force aerobatics team, The Thunderbirds, perform in their F-16s. In the world of pilots, they are real celebrities.

I can testify that precision formation flying through those intricate maneuvers requires almost uncanny skill and concentration, and as a young pilot, I used to dream about being on The Thunderbirds team.

Yet, I know that they are but the most visible members of the team. On the ground there are about sixty other people supporting those pilots and their planes.

That realization was dramatized on the day of the air show by the announcement that one of the crew chiefs was a local man whose family had given the entire Thunderbird team a big potluck dinner the night before. The crowd responded with a rousing cheer, and for a few hours, the local man was a celebrity in his own right. A good thing.

And it would be a good thing if, in a society in which we are drawn to celebrities and tend to imbue them with traits and characteristics and talents they don't possess, we would be sensitive to the different roles of the celebrities and the often unsung heroes.

To be sure, celebrities may be heroes and vice versa (General Schwarzkopf comes to mind), but more and more it seems to me that we bestow celebrityhood on anyone whose name is in the paper more than three times, regardless of the reason, and who may be anything *but* a hero (criminals such as John Gotti and Amy Fisher come to mind).

As a manager, it is important to recognize the difference and give each its due. In my business, magazine publishing, the editors generally are the celebrities. That's okay. But magazine executives also must honor and reward the people behind (and in some cases significantly supporting) the celebrity editors.

Every business has this dichotomy between the celebrities and the unsung heroes. In sales, the salespeople get the glory (and the pay), and the sales research and promotion people do the grunt work.

I know of companies in which the product designers are the celebrities, but the production people are the real heroes in making an efficacious product from those designs.

My advice to managers always is, "Of course let the celebrities have their glory, doing their fancy aerobatics while people crane their necks watching, but don't you ever be seduced by celebrityhood and forget how much you need those unsung heroes."

Eating Humble Pie

During a long automobile ride a few weeks ago, my lawyer son Rick and I were airing our fears about the degeneration of a sense of community in America. I related that to the degeneration of the language by the pop culture and my concern that we are forgetting how to use English.

"It's not a big concern of mine, Dad," Rick said.

"Why not? As a master user of the language, surely you are offended by what you hear on TV and in the movies and on recordings."

"It hurts my ear sometimes," he said, "but I'm not offended."

Then he added, "Dad you sound like those guys at the Sorbonne, the self-appointed defenders of the French language. What they've found out is that the custodianship of the language resides with the people, not the grammarians and scholars."

Rick then told of how impressed he was at the vivid and colorful language used in testimony by some of his lower-income, inner-city clients: "They tell their stories more persuasively than any English professor could."

Then he delivered his *coup de grâce:* "More language can't hurt. Words are only the symbols, often inadequate, of how we feel and how we perceive the world to be. When you put the symbols together in different ways, who knows what you might discover?"

Then he paused before the final thrust.

"Surely, as a writer and poet, Dad, you know that's what poetry's all about."

He rested his case, and I had no rebuttal except to stand corrected and to understand at last that feeling of having parented a child now smarter than his dad.

Hypocrisy, Mendacity, and Drugs

Warning: This is the view of one businessman—me—and not his publisher, his family, or his friends.

It is time to redefine the "war on drugs," and it is past time to back up and take a long, hard look at what we in this society believe about this subject versus what we *say* we believe.

Let me start with an anecdote. A few years ago, I attended a meeting of prestigious businesspeople who were being urged to support the "drug-free America" initiative. First we saw the statistics about all the illegal drugs and how they were wreaking havoc on our young people. We saw how much money was being spent on those drugs. And we saw how difficult it was for law enforcement officials to stop the flow of drugs.

"The answer," we were told, "is in cutting the demand for illegal drugs." This was to be done by advertising and promotion, accompanied in some areas by a more active enforcement of the laws against casual users.

In essence, the presentation concentrated on two things: the fact that use of illegal drugs is a character flaw, and that illegal drugs generally are an issue of criminality.

After the meeting, we adjourned to an open bar where most of us drank legal drugs and about a third of us smoked legal drugs.

Time out! What's wrong with this picture?

No, I'm not singing that obvious old song about one drug being legal and another being illegal, and the difference having only to do with the preferences of those in power.

And this is not an essay about decriminalizing now-illegal drugs—although I do think the so-called war on drugs, despite publicity to the contrary, is being lost and has poured much-needed billions of dollars into highly ineffective interdiction of supplies.

This is simply a suggestion that we redefine this whole issue further away from the law enforcement and judicial systems (which now, as a result of the famous "war on drugs," are overburdened with petty drug cases) and closer to a more appropriate realm: the public health.

The statistics are clear enough: Over four hundred thousand people a year die of tobacco-caused diseases; another two hundred thousand die of alcohol-caused diseases; and who knows how many die, or are addicted to, legal prescription drugs. There seems to be no clear statistic about deaths from *illegal* drugs, but the last number I saw was *less than ten thousand.*

Now I ask you: Purely from a public health point of view, with which drugs do the problems lie?

The current administration is addressing the health costs of tobacco and alcohol, yet we continue to view illegal drugs for the most part as a law-enforcement cost. The reason is simple enough: That's where we spend most of our money.

So, what to do?

I am not deluded into thinking there are simple answers here. Clearly, illegal drug users commit a large number of crimes, many of them violent, in order to get money to support their drug use. Illegal drug suppliers engage in territorial warfare on our streets, often killing innocent bystanders. The need for good local law enforcement here is apparent.

But I would like to see us divert some of the federal "war on drugs" money away from interdiction and enforcement and into education. You see, I do believe the advertising and promotion efforts of the drug-free America folks has had an impact. And I believe a more concentrated educational advertising campaign, tightly directed to the appropriate audiences, and concerning the dangers of *all* drug use, legal and illegal, would have great impact.

Then I'd also divert some of that money into more free treatment for addicts through the Public Health Service.

Would these things eliminate drug use? Of course not. We'll never do that. Would these things result in the decreased use of both legal and illegal drugs? I believe so.

More important, in my view, we would be transcending our own double standard about what clearly is an enormous health—and health cost—problem by focusing our major efforts on education and prevention of all drug abuse—not just the street drugs.

Spare me the morality debates about legal versus illegal drugs. That debate becomes a mere technicality when you watch a loved one die of lung cancer or when you go through an alcohol rehabilitation program. Somehow at that point, the laws and the identities of the drug suppliers seem less relevant.

The Wisdom of the People

I was fortunate on a recent evening to have dinner with the chairman and chief executive officer of one of the world's largest financial information companies at its global human resource management conference, where I was to speak the next morning.

The conversation was enlightening and affirming in many ways, but I was particularly struck by how much faith he has in the down-the-line employees of his company, those whom some executives might think of as the uninformed little people.

This CEO, to the contrary, speaks of their wisdom and illustrates it by telling of the conversation with a group of employees about the appropriate time to fire someone.

"I asked them this," he said. "Let's say you are the coach of a football team and you have a tight end who just can't catch the ball. He seemed good enough when you hired him, but he just has not come along. The quarterback throws him the ball and he drops it. What do you do?"

The employees answered, "You give him more training."

"Good answer," said the CEO, "so then I said, 'Okay, so you train him, but he just doesn't have the knack of catching the ball. He's mediocre at best and is dragging down the team. What then?' "

The people answered, "You transfer him to another position."

"Another good answer and one that might work," said

the CEO, "but I wanted to press them further, so I said, 'Okay, you put him in another position, but he still does not do the job. He has not been able to develop his ability, or perhaps has lost his commitment to playing football. What then?' "

With no hesitation, they answered, "You have to take him off the team." And they went on to explain that the team would never be able to have a winning season with him on the team, and everybody would suffer.

In ending the story, the CEO smiled across the table at me. "Who says the people don't know how to make tough management decisions? I call it the wisdom of the so-called little people."

And I call that the wisdom of a top-notch CEO.

How About a
Termination Review Board?

The medical profession comes in for its share of criticism, but the doctors have one procedure which I think should be adapted for business: a board reviews surgeries and other procedures to assure compliance with standards.

What could be more threatening to the well-being of a person or a family than the loss of a job? Surely, only the most critical surgical procedures have a more far-reaching effect on a person's future.

A firing situation is usually complex; the issues are both ethical and legal, and the risks are great indeed, to the person who has been fired, to the manager, and to the company. Yet, the firing of an employee is too frequently left to a manager's own often self-invented way of doing it.

Most companies have a procedure, a method for making the paper trail that presumably will provide legal protection, but almost none of them concern themselves with methods for assuring that the termination was necessary in the first place. In addition, almost none of them provide any training in the actual execution of what I think should be called the "caring confrontation."

Let's face it: No manager has a lot of experience in firing people—or at least no manager should have *a lot* of experience in it.

So I suggest that companies focus on this subject, establishing a process of deliberation before the fact, guidelines for managers in the doing of the act, and then a termination review board to assure that everyone involved—the employee, the manager, and the company—was represented properly and protected properly.

I believe the review should start with a report by the manager who did the firing, then should examine the history of performance appraisals, records of conversations, memos, and so on. The steps taken to correct the situation should be retraced, and the severance and out-placement arrangements evaluated.

Obviously, employees can fail, but I believe that companies should assure that every reasonable step was taken to prevent the failure.

A further advantage of this process is that the company inculcates the attitude that there is no such thing as a *routine* firing. Ever.

Affirmation and Information

I once heard Anthony Burgess, the author and expert on linguistics and the development of language, suggest at a conference that most of what we said either was a lie or was not worth saying.

By example, he offered the sentence, "New York women are good-looking."

"That," he said, "is a lie."

The accurate sentence is, "Some New York women are good-looking."

"That," he said, "is so obvious, it is not worth saying."

At the time, this comment very much fit my own feelings that about 90 percent of everything said in meetings did not need to be said. It seemed to me that in most business meetings, we were always repeating ourselves, saying obvious things not worth saying, or mouthing old truths not worth repeating.

Then I came to a new understanding, one that was later reinforced with a story told by Dr. Fred Craddock, a wonderful preacher and professor of homiletics at a theological seminary. Dr. Craddock said that when he was first a young minister, he thought it important that he find a somewhat obscure scripture as the theme for his sermon, or find a familiar scripture and give it an obscure interpretation.

This would be new material, a chance for education and growth for his congregation. The only thing was, he admitted, they didn't seem particularly interested or engaged by the sermons.

Then Dr. Craddock visited a church pastored by one of his African American colleagues and heard great enthuasiasm from the congregation as his colleague preached basically the same old sermon. "Yes, tell it," the people shouted.

It occurred, somewhat as a revelation to Dr. Craddock, that people generally want to hear, and be affirmed in, what they already know, at least to a great extent.

The same is true in business. We meet and talk and talk, often with the major intent being to assure one another and to affirm and be affirmed in the shared knowledge or vision or mission.

So I came to understand that, contrary to Mr. Burgess's view, some things are indeed worth saying, again and again, as trivial and meaningless as they may seem on the surface.

The point is affirmation, not information.

My Last Word
on Pop Culture Restraint

Despite my real concerns about the stuff bombarding us from movie and television screens and airwaves, I always feel somewhat uncomfortable calling for restraint (as I explain in "A Cry of Frustration" on page 159).

Then comes something like *Sliver*.

I shake my head at the coverage of everything surrounding this movie. Much of the big news emphasis has been on how clever the director was in editing the film so that he could just slip it into the *R* rating category.

I'd feel a lot better if entertainment businesspeople would engage the debate beyond all the chest-thumping about artistic freedom and the First Amendment.

Instead, we read the big stories on how far such and such a director was able to push the edge of the sex or violence envelope.

What an achievement. Just what the society needs these days: more people seeing how far they can stretch the system in order to make more bucks.

I am as close to a First Amendment absolutist as you will find outside the legal profession, but sometimes I feel those of us active in First Amendment issues are going to find ourselves desperately trying to plug the dike as a tidal wave of fed-up public concern washes us away.

So one more time: Wake up, my friends in the entertainment industry, it's getting later than you think!

Some Obvious Conclusions
About Health-Care Costs

It now seems conventional wisdom that stress is a major cause of illness. By extension, then, stress is a major cause of health-care costs.

Company executives complain regularly about health-care costs. They then take various steps to cut those costs: reducing or eliminating benefits, requiring copayments, or larger copayments by employees, and so on.

What very few company executives ever seem to think about is how the working environment creates stress, thus contributes to health-care costs. In fact, one senior manager told me, "I see part of my job description as *creating* stess."

I have introduced the subject of stress into many management discussions and have pointed out that we know how to reduce stress. There are dozens of techniques. "Why," I have asked, "do more companies not bring those techniques right into the workplace, thus creating a lower stress level and creating a healthier working environment?"

The answer usually has something to do with the desire to wait and see how this works for the companies that are trying it. This attitude dismisses altogether the view that a healthier, lower stress environment also contributes to employee morale and productivity.

I think also that some executives view the methods of stress reduction as diversions that will take people's attention away from their work or will cost extra money.

The upshot of these attitudes, combined with an atmosphere in which layoffs and downward pressure on wages and benefits frequently dominate the news, is that most companies continue to increase rather than decrease stress.

This, however, does not stop them from complaining about the increase in health-care costs and does not stop their doomsday predictions about government intervention.

Reconsidering
the Carrot and the Stick

Some managers believe that it is bad technique to give a raise or a bonus and, at the same time, deliver criticism to the employee receiving those rewards.

If you're one of those managers, abandon that thought immediately.

A raise or a bonus are rewards for a job well done and for goals achieved. They are not necessarily rewards for a job *perfectly* done.

While I have known managers who seemed unable to deliver a compliment, raise, or bonus without also adding an often gratuitous "Yeah, but you should have . . . " I have more often seen managers who could not deliver complaints or criticism.

What better time to review performance, to criticize, and to articulate expectations for the future than when you can say, in effect, "You are a person of accomplishment as evidenced by this raise (or bonus), so as I congratulate you, I also want to express some disappointment and tell you how you could have made your accomplishment even better, and how you can do so in the coming year."

Think of it this way: When you hand people money, you generally have their undivided attention.

Another Way to Think About a Job Change

As I was preparing myself emotionally and psychologically to retire from my position as a senior corporate executive to become a writer and consultant, I expressed my concern to Joey Rodger of the Public Library Association.

She gave me a wonderful way to think about it:

"Clearly, in my opinion," she said, "what you are doing is *leaving the obviously good for the somehow strangely better.*"

Yes.

Four Important Things
in Life and Work

Find your people.
Find your place.
Tell your story.
Listen.

An Epitaph We Could
All Be Proud Of

I have always had a lot of trouble allowing people to do things for me.

"It's an old childhood fear," I once told Sally, "that I would be beholden to someone, as we said then—that someone would have something on me."

"Oh, that's important," she laughed. "Just think. On your tombstone they can write, 'Here lies Jim Autry. Nobody had anything on him.'"

Her epitaph put the whole problem in perspective for me, while at the same time making me laugh. What a wonderful idea, I thought, to measure all our ideals and foibles by how they'd look as an epitaph on a tombstone.

Since then, I have incorporated the writing of one's own epitaph into my management workshops. I ask the participants to write down how they would want to be remembered. "Be serious or humorous, as you wish," I say. "Perhaps one approach is to write your own epitaph. What would you want your tombstone to say to those people who visit your grave years from now?"

You'd be amazed at the results, and more important, you'd be amazed at the discussions this exercise provokes. Once people begin thinking about their own deaths, other things fall into perspective.

As one workshop participant said, "I'll bet no one writes, 'Here lies Joe Blow. He died wishing he'd spent more time at the office.'"

The most memorable, and most moving, self-written epitaph came from Matt Handbury, managing director of Murdoch Magazines in Sydney, Australia, who was participating in the session with his own employees. So this one took a very large amount of self-awareness and courage. It read:

Here lies Matt.
He wasn't.
And then he wasn't some more, though he thought otherwise.
And then he was and is.
And others were also, the more through and with him
And together they did things better than otherwise might have been.
And that is, and is enough.

Can you imagine the thrill I felt, as leader of this workshop, to be rewarded by so moving, insightful, and self-examining an effort?

And can you imagine a better epitaph for any of us, regardless of our calling?

Index